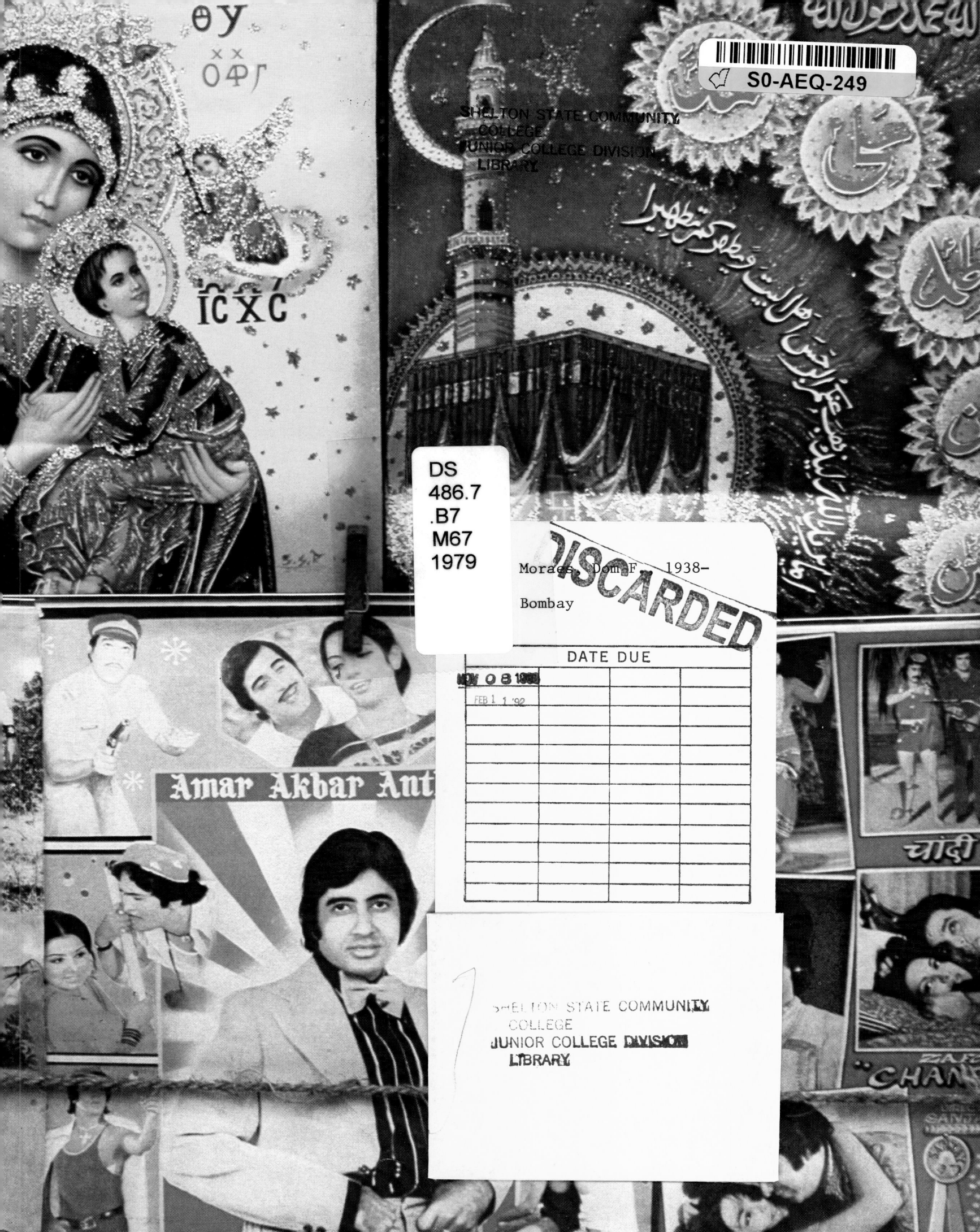

BOMBAY

By Dom Moraes
and the Editors of Time-Life Books

Photographs by Bruno Barbey

THE GREAT CITIES · TIME-LIFE BOOKS · AMSTERDAM

The Author: Born in 1938, Dom Moraes was educated in Bombay and at Oxford University. In 1958 he became the youngest ever recipient of the Hawthornden Award for his volume of poems *A Beginning*. He has travelled extensively in the Third World and has received awards for his reporting and for his TV scripts. His published works include volumes of poetry, an autobiography, and a book on world population problems commissioned by the United Nations Organization.

The Photographer: Bruno Barbey was born in 1941 in Morocco, and began his photographic career in 1960. Since joining Magnum Photos in 1966, he has covered stories all over the world. In addition to being a frequent contributor to international periodicals, including LIFE, *Stern* and *Geo Magazine*, his work has appeared in major exhibitions in France, Britain and Switzerland.

THE SEAFARERS
WORLD WAR II
THE GOOD COOK
THE TIME-LIFE ENCYCLOPAEDIA
OF GARDENING
HUMAN BEHAVIOUR
THE GREAT CITIES
THE ART OF SEWING
THE OLD WEST
THE WORLD'S WILD PLACES
THE EMERGENCE OF MAN
LIFE LIBRARY OF PHOTOGRAPHY
THIS FABULOUS CENTURY
TIME-LIFE LIBRARY OF ART
FOODS OF THE WORLD
GREAT AGES OF MAN
LIFE SCIENCE LIBRARY
LIFE NATURE LIBRARY
YOUNG READERS LIBRARY
LIFE WORLD LIBRARY
THE TIME-LIFE BOOK OF BOATING
TECHNIQUES OF PHOTOGRAPHY
LIFE AT WAR
LIFE GOES TO THE MOVIES
BEST OF LIFE

TIME-LIFE INTERNATIONAL
EUROPEAN EDITOR: Kit van Tulleken
Design Director: Louis Klein
Photography Director: Pamela Marke
Chief of Research: Vanessa Kramer
Text Director: Simon Rigge (acting)
Chief Designer: Graham Davis
Chief Sub-Editor: Ilse Gray

THE GREAT CITIES
Series Editor: Deborah Thompson
Editorial Staff for *Bombay*
Text Editor: Jeremy Lawrence
Designers: Derek Copsey, Joyce Mason
Picture Editor: Gunn Brinson
Staff Writers: Mike Brown, Anthony Masters
Text Researcher: Milly Trowbridge
Sub-Editor: Nicoletta Flessati
Design Assistant: Susan Altman
Editorial Assistants: Stephanie Lindsay, Katie Lloyd

Editorial Production
Production Editor: Ellen Brush
Traffic Co-ordinators: Pat Boag, Joanne Holland
Picture Department: Catherine Lewes, Belinda Stewart Cox
Art Department: Julia West
Editorial Department: Ajaib Singh Gill

The captions and the texts accompanying the photographs in this volume were prepared by the editors of TIME-LIFE Books.

Published by TIME-LIFE International (Nederland) B.V. Ottho Heldringstraat 5, Amsterdam 1018.

ISBN 7054 0497 8

Cover: A throng celebrating the festival of the elephant-headed Hindu deity Ganesh crowds a street in central Bombay. In the densely populated city the number of participants in the annual procession runs into millions.

First end paper: At a street-corner stall, inexpensive posters of religious images—Hindu, Muslim and Christian alike—share a display with pin-ups of some of the stars of Bombay's flourishing film industry.

Last end paper: On the seashore near Malabar Hill, bone-white washing is draped on rocks to dry. The public laundry area is known as Dhobi Ghats or the "laundry steps". Bombay's *dhobis* (washermen) rely on cold water and sun-bleaching to achieve a spotless finish for the clothes they wash.

Contents

I

The Gateway of India

When I was a child in Bombay, I was continually aware that we were surrounded by water. A couple of hundred yards from my parents' flat was the Arabian Sea, whose tall waves shattered themselves on the sea wall when the monsoons thundered up behind them. I had an imaginary picture of the provenance of these waves, drawn from the name of the sea: I dreamt that they had swept to the west coast of India from some wild and sandy shore, where armed bedouins on camels watched them from the dunes. Inland, when my parents and I drove out of the city for our Sunday picnics, we encountered more water: muddy tidal creeks sticky with mangroves, and huge lakes rippled by crocodiles.

My childhood memories are full of the smell and feel of so much water. Its pervasive presence was scarcely remarkable, since what is now Bombay once consisted of an archipelago of seven swampy and malarial islands inhabited by aboriginal fishermen known as Kolis; where the bare-breasted Koli women waded into the surf to help unload returning fishing-boats, there now stands the most prosperous commercial city in the whole of India.

Bombay is a gritty, impossible, unforgettable place. It has child beggars, pavement sleepers and sprawling urban slums; noise, tangled traffic, skyscrapers, fashionable apartment blocks; the very poor, who have migrated from villages in the surrounding regions to seek better fortune; and the very rich—merchants, industrialists, film stars. It is also, in a very special sense, India's most cosmopolitan city. The Indian subcontinent is the home of peoples as diverse, ethnically and in terms of language and custom, as those of all the countries of Europe put together; and no city is more representative of this diversity than Bombay, to which people from almost all parts of the country have gravitated.

In 1665 the British took possession of Bombay, over which they exercised a hegemony that lasted till India's independence in 1947. By the time that the first small British community was established in Bombay, five of the original seven islands were already interconnected at low tide by shallow sandbanks, silted up over the years. The two small, southernmost ones—known to the British as Old Woman's Island and Colaba—were likewise joined by a sandbar, but divided from the others by a deep channel. By 1730 land reclamation, carried out under the supervision of the British, had permanently united the five islands into a single mass, and large earthworks had been thrown up to prevent major invasion by the sea of the low-lying interior. A hundred years later a causeway was built to link the

At dusk Bombayites in shirt-sleeves or colourful saris stroll beside the Gateway of India, which faces out across Bombay Harbour. Erected to commemorate the state visit in 1911 of King George V, Emperor of India, the arch stands on Apollo Bunder, the principal quay for passengers arriving in India when it was ruled by Britain.

city to the two straggling islands lying to the south, and central Bombay was at last recognizably the same entity that it is today.

On a map, the site of the present-day city appears as a claw-like promontory, some 12 miles long, that hangs, pointing south, from the west coast of India. At its northern end it is linked by several road and rail bridges to a very much larger island, Salsette, that is itself similarly connected to the Indian mainland across the Ulhas River to the north, and Thana Creek to the east. (Most of Salsette now falls within the municipal limits of Greater Bombay, which covers about 240 square miles.) Eastwards from Bombay Island lies a great natural harbour—unrivalled anywhere else on the subcontinent—that provides 75 square miles of sheltered, deep water. Beyond that spreads the mainland of India.

The twin talons or claws of the promontory consist of two peninsulas that enclose between them the sweeping curve of Back Bay. Malabar Hill, on the western peninsula, is one of Bombay's most exclusive residential areas. Here and on the adjacent Cumballa Hill were situated the ornate and enormous homes built by wealthy industrialists in the 19th Century and the early years of the 20th; since the 1950s most of these mansions have been bulldozed into the red earth to provide space for skyscraper apartment blocks that rent at exorbitant prices. Reaching around the curve of the bay is a boulevard, Marine Drive, whose lights, brightly gleaming after the brief dusk has fallen, are known locally as the Queen's Necklace. They are seen at their best from the Hanging Gardens: a public park, famous for its topiary hedges, that was laid out in 1881 on Malabar Hill. Glittering against the bosom of the sea, the great electric necklace looped over three miles of the bay is one of Bombay's more memorable sights.

Across the bay from Malabar is the longer peninsula of Colaba; it came into being as a result of the joining of the two southernmost islands and subsequent land reclamation—an ambitious government project, begun in the early 1960s and known as the Back Bay Reclamation. On Colaba the British built what they called cantonments (pronounced "cantoonments"): white colonial houses for the officers, brick barracks for the troops, and shade trees lining the avenues. Here also is St. John's Church, consecrated in 1858 and popularly known as the Afghan Church because it is dedicated to British soldiers who were killed in the Afghan campaigns of 1838 to 1842. The area still contains an Indian military base, though today it is overshadowed by the immense apartment and office blocks that have been erected on part of the Back Bay Reclamation.

Due north of Colaba lies the commercial heart of the city, the Fort area. Named after the British fortifications that stood here from the late 17th Century until the 1860s, this district is cluttered with traffic, people, shops and restaurants, modern offices and banks. Some of its older buildings, of the late 19th and early 20th Centuries, combine elements of Victorian Gothic design with those of a characteristic "Indo-Saracenic" style that

Two women sort fresh prawns at the edge of the Back Bay Reclamation, where a stretch of water near the city's southern tip is gradually being reclaimed for new construction. On the further shore, on land already reclaimed from the sea, rise tower blocks of luxury apartments.

derived from Arabic influences. Three adjoining *maidans*, or stretches of parkland—the Oval, the Cross Maidan and the Azad Maidan—provide a belt of greenery running from south to north through the centre of the city. Another monument of the Victorian era stands at the centre of the Fort: Flora Fountain, an ornate structure in dull stone decorated at its four corners with mythological figures and topped by a representation of Flora, the Roman goddess of flowers. Erected in honour of a British Governor of the city, Sir Bartle Frere, it was placed in position in 1869 at the conjunction of five broad thoroughfares.

Once, the vicinity of Flora Fountain was also adorned with marble statues of British monarchs, Bombay governors and civil servants. But after British colonial rule ended in 1947, India became an independent federal republic, with Delhi as its capital and Bombay the capital of one of the states that made up the federation; and, in an uprush of nationalist feeling following these developments, many hideous civic statues of British notables were removed from the Fort area. For a while their plinths were empty, providing beds of a kind for some of the city's homeless population: ever-present unfortunates who are obliged to sleep in Bombay's streets. Alas, the reason for the removal of the statues was not aesthetic: the government of the state replaced the original sculptures with statues of Indian folk heroes and politicians—if anything even less beautiful, to my eye, than their colonial predecessors.

The Fort is flanked to the north by a belt of thriving markets or bazaars that sell everything from essential foodstuffs to luxuries like perfumes, jewellery and antique furniture. Beyond the bazaars, Bombay Island is one great urban sprawl of densely crowded tenements; slum areas that the government of the state has been promising, ever since Independence, to pull down and replace with proper housing; factories and cotton mills puffing smoke from pipe-stemmed chimneys; railway lines and monotonous streets running north and south.

Bombay is a linear city; its suburbs trail northwards across Mahim Creek, the tidal inlet that marks the boundary between Bombay Island and Salsette, and continue to unfold for another 30 miles. From these dormitory communities more than a million people flock south to the city centre every working day. They are served by two parallel railway systems ending at Churchgate Station, near the Oval in the Fort area, and at Victoria Terminus, invariably referred to by the local population as "V.T." A Victorian Gothic edifice which stylistically rivals the architectural fantasy of London's St. Pancras Station, Victoria Terminus lies to the east of the Azad Maidan and is said to have been erected over what was once the chief shrine of Mumba (or Mumbai) Devi, the mother goddess worshipped by the Kolis.

In the great harbour east of the Fort many ships lie at anchor in water that is blue most of the year but churned to muddy yellow during the monsoon season, from June to September. As a rule, the ships stand off in deep water, well away from the shore, waiting their turn to moor at one or other of the docks that line the east coast of Bombay Island. Bombay is by far the largest and busiest port of India, handling twice the tonnage of her two closest competitors, Calcutta and Cochin. Two-thirds of the country's shipping companies have their headquarters here. Here too, at Mazagaon Dock, is India's leading shipbuilding and ship-repair yard.

A series of *bunders*, or piers, protrudes into the harbour, the oldest of these being Apollo Bunder. (It does not derive its name from the Greek god but—according to one explanation—from a local fish, the *palla*, that used to be landed here in great numbers.) In the heyday of the British Raj, passengers from Europe would disembark at Apollo Bunder and, though only harbour launches make use of it today (deep-water piers to the north and south now receive the ocean-going traffic), that era is recalled by a triumphal arch erected here to commemorate the arrival of King George V and Queen Mary on a state visit in 1911. Constructed of yellow basalt and completed in 1924, the massive arch is known as the Gateway of India. Perched at the end of the *bunder*, it serves no practical purpose but is regarded as a symbol of Bombay itself.

On the Colaba sea front facing the Gateway stands the Taj Mahal Hotel, opened in 1903. It was financed by Jamsetjee Tata, a member of the family that to this day rules one of India's biggest industrial empires. The "Taj" was the first building recognized by sea voyagers as they approached the city, and in all the Far East its fame is coeval with that of two other historic hostelries: the Peninsula in Hong Kong and Raffles in Singapore. The British disembarking from the newly moored liners would immediately take refuge in its bar, under its electric ceiling fans; if they were to take up posts in India, potential servants would approach them there to offer their services—while, on the road outside, beggars moaned as softly as the fans did.

I think it was in the Taj's Rendezvous restaurant that, at the age of 15, I dined out as man to man with my father for the first time. As I recall, the Rendezvous in those days—the early 1950s—had a large placard outside it reading "No dogs or South Africans admitted"—a gesture of retaliation provoked by South Africa's then recent apartheid legislation that discriminated against that country's Indian population. When, in the course of our lunch, we discussed plans for my education, my father said: "By the way, I've never asked you what you want to do after Oxford. We ought to work it out, you know."

I told him I wanted to try to write—both poetry and prose. "Well, at least you are definite," he said. "But where do you want to do all this?"

I replied without hesitation: "Not in this city."

"I've lived a lot of my life here," my father said. "It's not all that bad. Bombay will survive, because it is tough; in twenty years it will become

In Versova, one of the fishing villages in the city's northern suburbs, a fisherman repaints the eyes on his boat's prow. According to local tradition, the boats are holy and, if given eyes, can sight shoals of fish. Fishing was the chief livelihood of the settlement of Bombay when England acquired it in the 17th Century.

a kind of small New York City. You'll probably see it happen, even if I don't. Bombay will be the city that dominates the country."

I replied that I didn't necessarily want to live in India at all. He shrugged his shoulders and said: "It's your life." Then, to my amazement, he quoted a verse of Kipling:

> *"I am the land of their fathers,*
> *In me the virtue stays;*
> *I will bring back my children*
> *After certain days."*

I did not have much to say in reply, so I was silent; but the verse remained in my head, along with my memory of the atmosphere of the Rendezvous: hermetically sealed against dogs and South Africans—and against any native Indian who did not earn at least as much in a month as most Bombayites earned in a year.

Part of what my father prophesied for Bombay has come true. By now it does resemble a not-so-small New York City. Its population has reached an estimated eight million. Like New Yorkers, the citizens of Bombay have some indefinable but perceptible quality that makes them easily identifiable to their own countrymen. Had I not left Bombay a few short steps beyond my childhood, I would probably be a totally different person from the one I have become. This capacity for imprinting its identity upon its inhabitants is, to me, the hallmark of a great city.

Remnants of Bombay's early history can still be seen in and around the city, perhaps most remarkably in the continuing presence of the Kolis: the short, dark-skinned people who were the earliest known inhabitants of the seven islands. Colaba, today the name given to the part of Bombay that lies south of the Fort, is derived from "Koli"—as is the word "coolie" in the sense of a labourer hired for a pittance.

There are several Koli fishing communities on the west coast of Salsette. The little village at Madh, for instance, cannot have changed much over the centuries, though the fishermen's big wooden boats, once propelled by oars, are now also fitted with engines, and their hulls may be filled with ice to preserve the catch—so that they can travel faster and further than they were able to do before.

In the early morning the village huts, many still built of mud and pebble, empty themselves. Naked children prance over a beach adorned with shells of curious shapes and colours, and with the bubble-like excavations of tiny crabs. The tide seeps in and with it come the boats, floating in from a still-indistinct horizon. The Koli women awaiting the landings wear their traditional, uniquely arranged saris: hitched up to the knees and twisted between the thighs. Unlike their ancestors, however, they now also wear blouses; and some of them can afford to adorn their splendid bodies with gold ornaments. Their valuable necklaces, bracelets and anklets seem out of place, considering the simplicity of their costume and the strenuous manual work that they do: lifting the fully laden baskets from the reeking boats. But then, as Bombay's population swells and with it the demand for fish, the Koli communities on Salsette have been growing increasingly prosperous as a result of their traditional activities.

There were other inhabitants of the island archipelago in the early days: the lighter-skinned Bhandaris, whose name is derived from the Sanskrit for "distiller". Both they and the Kolis were hard drinkers of liquor, brewed either from palm sap or rice. The Bhandaris' main occupation—other than distillation of these liquors—seems to have been the cultivation of rice (for which the swampy conditions were admirably suitable) as well as raising other types of vegetables.

At Kanheri on Salsette Island sacred stone carvings provide valuable evidence about later visitors to the area. There is a wooded hill, at the end of a long valley, whose flanks are riddled with caves; and in the two largest of these are representations of the Buddha that were shaped from the native rock somewhere between the 3rd and 9th Centuries A.D. When I was young, I used to cross the dusty valley on foot or by bullock-cart, having descended from one of the crowded trains that ran from the city. On reaching the hill, I would look down at the forested ravines on the other side of the valley and be deeply moved, knowing that so many centuries before me the men who carved the figures—shaven monks in their yellow robes—had gazed over the same scene when they paused from chopping and hacking at the stone. In the smaller caves this same troglodyte Buddhist community had cut rough couches out of the rock; and on these they slept, perhaps cushioned against too many bruises by

In the late 18th Century, when this engraving was first published, some low-lying areas of Bombay's site were still inundated at each high tide. The view embraces what is today, after extensive reclamation from the sea, the continuous shore of Back Bay. The tower of St. Thomas' Church, now a cathedral, dominates the town on the left; the lighthouse at Colaba is on the extreme right; and the mainland of India lies in the background.

grass mats. They also constructed an elaborate drainage system, the flues and vents of which carried down the hill the excess water of the monsoons and, I suppose, the sewage.

The island of Elephanta lies in Bombay Harbour, an hour's journey by motor launch from Apollo Bunder. There a later community—in this case, Hindu—constructed a huge complex of temples and statues, thought by some authorities to date from the 6th Century A.D. Everything was carved out of the living rock within the labyrinth of caves that navel one of the island's two hills. Once, the stone gods and goddesses here were garlanded and painted with turmeric by their chanting worshippers. Today, unadorned and battered by the centuries, they are quite casually acknowledged by tourists. The Hindus who originally worshipped here were devotees of the god Shiva and the most famous of the island's sculptures is the so-called *Maheshamurti*: a three-headed bust of Shiva, 18 feet high, that depicts him in three of his divine aspects. The great elephant carved in black stone that gave the island its name was removed in 1864, some years after its head had fallen off, to preserve it from further dilapidation; it now stands—reassembled in one piece—in Victoria Gardens, a park in the centre of Bombay Island.

Elephanta—or Gharapuri (Fortress City), as the island is locally known —owes the creation of its temple complex to a revival of orthodox Hinduism in western India that followed a decline of its offshoot, Buddhism, from the 6th Century A.D. On the adjacent mainland area of Maharashtra ("Great Kingdom" in Sanskrit) a succession of Hindu dynasties arose. Some of these were established by indigenous Marathi-speakers, but others were set up by Kannada-speaking rulers who made incursions from further

south. By 1300 one of these rulers, known as King Bhimadeva or Bimba, had settled his capital at Mahim, one of the original seven islands and the name of a Bombay suburb today.

In the 14th Century, Muslim invaders from the north demolished Bimba's capital. Writing in the 1320s, two Italian friars, Jordanus and Odoric, missionaries who for three years lived in Thana at the head of the creek of that name, noted that: "The Saracens hold the whole country, having lately usurped the dominion. They have destroyed an infinite number of idol temples." The friars also recorded that the mainland was full of "black lions" (possibly panthers) and rhinoceroses: clearly this was still wild country, made even more savage by pitched battles between Hindus and the conquering Muslims.

In the 16th Century the Muslims yielded, in their turn, to the superior force of Portuguese colonists. By 1498 the Portuguese navigator Vasco da Gama had discovered the sea route to India via the Cape of Good Hope. By a treaty signed in 1534 the Portuguese acquired the trading station of Bassein (just north of Salsette) and its dependencies, including Salsette itself and the seven islands. The archipelago was named *Bom Bahia*, or "Good Bay", to which may be traced the derivation of the city's present name. But there are two other theories on that score. Some linguistic scholars hold that "Bombay" is a distortion of "Bimba", the name of the early King; while others—in the explanation most widely supported today —believe the city's name to be a corruption of "Mumbai", the tutelary goddess worshipped by the Kolis.

Early in the 17th Century the British arrived in India to trade and immediately came into conflict with the Portuguese. Fifty years later the British acquired Bombay not by force but as a gift. The islands were included as part of the dowry of the Portuguese princess, the Infanta Catharine of Braganza, when she married King Charles II of England in 1661. This present was strenuously opposed by the Viceroy of the Portuguese colony of Goa, 250 miles south of Bombay; he was a man of common sense who could see a bright commercial future for the harbour. When the British arrived to take official possession of the islands, their troops were detained for no less than two and a half years in the malarial swamps of Angedive Island, just south of Goa, while their commander, Sir Abraham Shipman, repeatedly tried to parley with the intransigent Viceroy. When at last Bombay was handed over peacefully in February, 1665, the original British force—some 400 strong—had been all but wiped out by disease: only 120 remained. Shipman, appointed to be Bombay's first British Governor, had died the year before.

Under the British—when they finally established themselves—Bombay was eventually to fulfil the potential foreseen for the city and its harbour by the Portuguese Viceroy. It was a slow process. During the 18th Century,

Lit up in the evening, Marine Drive—Bombay's main promenade, overlooking Back Bay—lives up to its popular local nickname: the Queen's Necklace, a reference to the chain of lights along the sea front. Behind the ocean-front apartment blocks are a hockey stadium (top) and Brabourne Stadium (right), one of the grounds where international cricket is played.

the city gradually developed as a trading station; but then, from about 1830 onwards, a much more rapid industrial and commercial expansion took place. The growing prosperity, together with the religious tolerance shown by the British, attracted to the city immigrants from all over the Indian subcontinent and beyond.

The neighbouring Marathas provided a labour force. Shrewd business-men from the province of Gujarat, north of Bombay, came to make their fortunes. Parsis—a Zoroastrian community that had fled from Persia in the 8th Century because of Muslim persecution—moved down to Bombay from Gujarat, where they had first settled. The surnames that some Parsis now bear have little relation to their original ones; instead they reflect the trades in which they became engaged in Bombay: names like Engineer or Contractor or Commissariat.

Muslims, too, came from Persia as well as from the Konkan (the coastal belt stretching southward from Bombay), from Goa and elsewhere. Then there were the Jains—mostly from Rajasthan and Gujarat—who are members of a small but influential sect that split off from Hinduism in early times; and colonies of Jews, Armenians, Sikhs and Chinese. In 1947 a large influx was added to this mixed community: Hindu refugees from the province of Sind in Pakistan, who had been displaced after the departure of the British by the partition of the subcontinent into the separate nations of India and Pakistan.

These millions of settlers who flooded into Bombay in succeeding centuries helped to make it not only the most cosmopolitan city in India, but also the wealthiest. Bombay yields about a third of India's income-tax revenue, and some two-fifths of all the country's revenue from air- and sea-borne trade. It has the country's busiest stock exchange and the largest concentration of industries. About a third of the city's employed popula-tion is engaged in manufacturing and a quarter in trade and commerce. Nowadays the manufactured goods—such as textiles, plastic products, and electrical and electronic equipment—that are produced in Bombay's factories are shipped not only to other parts of India but also to the booming oil states of the Arabian peninsula, to Iran and Iraq, to Europe and the United States.

To meet the rising traffic in foreign trade, the city's port facilities have been continually expanded and improved. The result is a string of wharves on Bombay's harbour front, from Sassoon Dock south of the Taj Mahal Hotel to Timber Bunder in the north. In 1944, during the Second World War, a large part of this dock area was shattered by a cataclysmic explosion when an ammunition ship blew up. Had the ammunition dumps on the docks been ignited, half the city would probably have been blown to pieces. Great comets of flame rushed over the Bombay sky and quenched them-selves in the sea. They happened to rush over me and my *ayah* (nanny), who was taking me for a walk on Marine Drive at the time. I told the

Policemen do their early morning exercises in front of the old Taj Mahal Hotel, now linked to a modern wing that stands, unseen, to the right. Overlooking the harbour, the Taj became a world-wide attraction when it opened in 1903 because of its grandeur: it had a granite staircase, 400 bedrooms and electric ceiling fans.

Flora Fountain, in front of the ornate Public Works Secretariat, marks a junction of five streets that is to Bombay what Piccadilly Circus is to London. Topped by a figure of the goddess Flora, the fountain was built in 1869 and paid for by a wealthy Bombay merchant to honour a former Governor, Sir Bartle Frere.

ayah that we had better get back home, but she had different ideas. She drew out her rosary (she belonged to Bombay's Catholic community), knelt and started to tell her beads, under the impression that this was the end of the world. Quite soon we were rescued by my mother, who arrived in our car, swept us into it and took us home. Then she went to the harbour to see if she could help, for she was a doctor. Indeed, large numbers of people rushed in the same direction and the fire was eventually squelched into cold ash.

Now, on any clear night, walking along the pavement that connects the Gateway of India to the Radio Club (a fashionable social club) about 200 yards southwards, one can see the gleaming decklights of the dozens of ships that are always waiting their turn to berth. A network of railways owned by the Port Trust Authority links all the docks to the city's two main railway stations, providing access to the vast hinterland.

The movement of materials from Bombay on such a large scale within and outside the country requires the presence of financing, broking, insuring and shipping facilities. And it was to perform these services that, over the generations, a complex of banks, broking agencies, insurance companies, and shipping and trucking firms grew up in the city. In the Fort area, where most of these businesses are located, there are streets called Bank Street and Dalal (Broker) Street; and one of the main roads is named after the Old Customs House, a relic of colonial times. There is, of course, a new Customs House, not very far from the old one. It stands facing the sea at Ballard Pier, nowadays a main point of disembarkation for ship passengers.

The commodity that the customs officers of British days most concerned themselves with was cotton—grown in the black soil of Gujarat and Maharashtra and exported to England to feed the textile mills of Lancashire and Yorkshire. Today cotton bales are also shipped *into* the port from countries such as Egypt and the Sudan; the number of textile mills in Bombay has grown to such an extent that the indigenous production of cotton is not enough to satisfy their demand. Thus, cotton retains its traditional importance to the city; and the feverish activity that goes on at the Cotton Exchange, situated a couple of miles north of Victoria Terminus, is the standing (some would say shouting) evidence.

The city's commercial significance was recognized early on by the British, and so when it was decided to establish a Reserve Bank of India they chose Bombay for its site. The R.B.I., as it is commonly called, is the central bank of the country and is used by the government to regulate the rate at which banknotes are printed, and thus to control the money supply. Both inwardly and outwardly, it is modelled on the Bank of England in London. Its grey stone building, completed in 1935, has the solid, sombre appearance of its London counterpart. It stands at the junction of Mint Road and Horniman Circle, like a sentinel keeping a watchful eye on the

Timber
Bunder

SEWRI

COTTON
GREEN

DADAR

Mills

Mills

Mills

● Haffkine
Institute

Mills

Mills

PAREL

● Portuguese
Church

Mills

Mills

Mills

Mills

Mahim Bay

WORLI

Buddhist ●
Temple

Dr. Annie Besant Road

ARABIAN SEA

Docks

Mazagaon
Dock

Prince's
Dock

Vict
D

Frere Road

Dockyard Road

MAZAGAON

Reay Road

Mills

Bhendi ●
Bazaar

Raudat Taher
Mausoleum

●Victoria and
Albert Museum

*Victoria
Gardens*

● Gloria Church

BHULESHWA

● Chor Bazaar

Sir J. J. Road

BYCULLA

NAGPADA

N. M. Joshi Road

KAMATIPURA

Mills

Foras Road

Grant Road

Sardar Patel

●Bombay Central
Station

Mahalakshmi Race
Course

● Willingdon
Sports Club

CUMBALLA HILL

Pedder Road **Tower of Sile**

Mahalakshmi Temple

●Breach
Candy Baths

Haji Ali Tomb

Burgeoning Harbour City

Located on the largest deep-water harbour
on India's west coast, Bombay is the country's
biggest and busiest port. The claw-shaped
promontory on which the modern city stands
has been built up by land reclamation over
the centuries from a string of seven small,
low-lying, coastal islands.

The city centre, with its markets, public
buildings, rail terminals and cotton mills, is
concentrated in the area of the original
islands (main map, above). But with Bombay's huge growth in population—from 2.5
million in 1947 to more than eight million—
the city has expanded haphazardly northwards through Salsette Island, prompting
civic plans to divert development to a new
"Twin City" eastwards across the harbour
(inset map, far right).

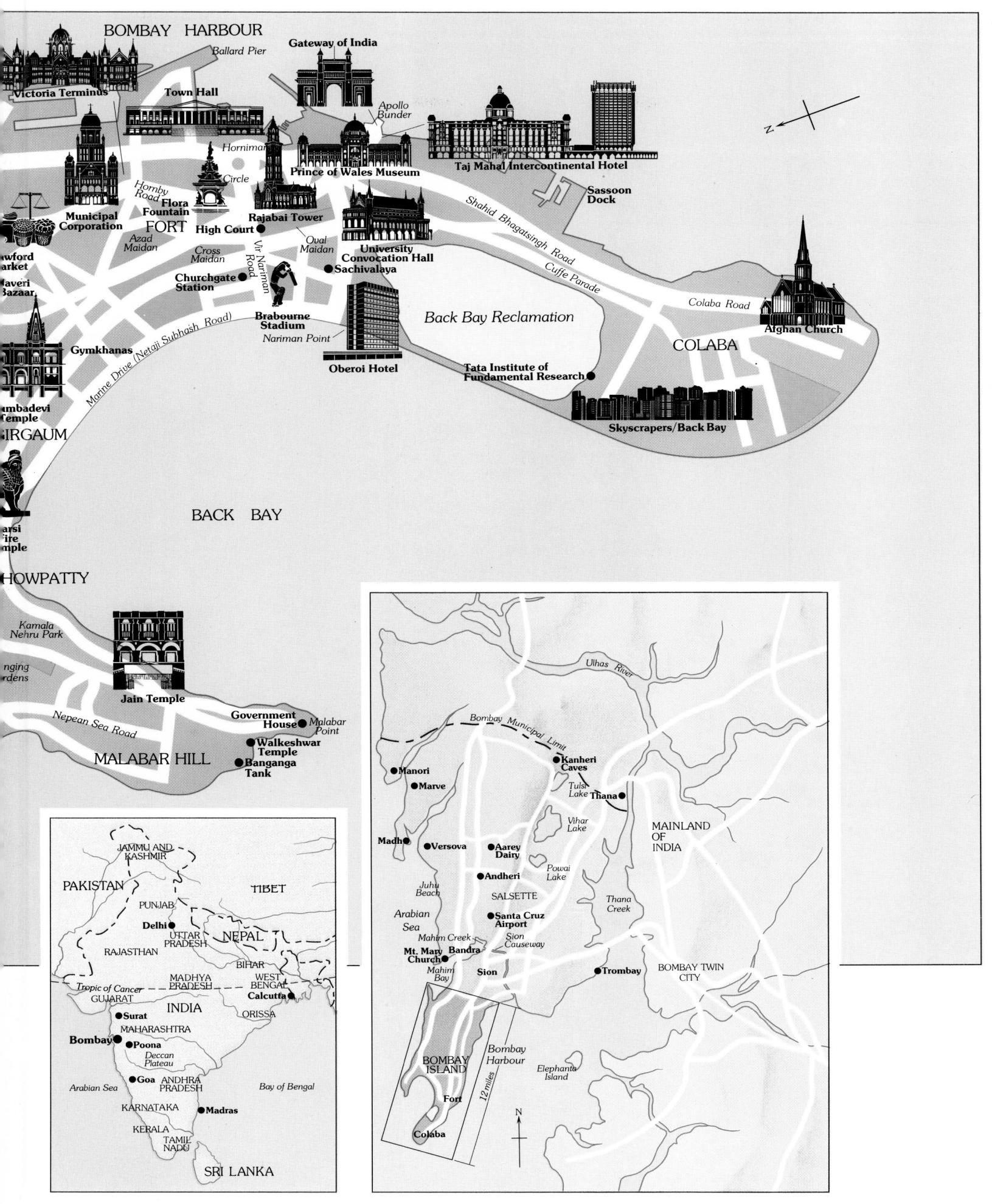

BOMBAY HARBOUR

Ballard Pier

Gateway of India

Victoria Terminus

Town Hall

Apollo Bunder

Horniman Circle

Prince of Wales Museum

Taj Mahal Intercontinental Hotel

Sassoon Dock

Hornby Road

Flora Fountain

Municipal Corporation

FORT

High Court

Rajabai Tower

Azad Maidan

Oval Maidan

Cross Maidan

Vir Nariman Road

University Convocation Hall

Sachivalaya

Shahid Bhagatsingh Road

Cuffe Parade

Colaba Road

Churchgate Station

Afghan Church

Brabourne Stadium

Back Bay Reclamation

COLABA

Gymkhanas

Marine Drive (Netaji Subhash Road)

Nariman Point

Oberoi Hotel

Tata Institute of Fundamental Research

mbadevi Temple

IRGAUM

Skyscrapers/Back Bay

arsi ire mple

BACK BAY

HOWPATTY

Kamala Nehru Park

nging rdens

Jain Temple

Government House

Malabar Point

Nepean Sea Road

Walkeshwar Temple

MALABAR HILL

Banganga Tank

Ulhas River

Bombay Municipal Limit

Manori

Kanheri Caves

Marve

Tulsi Lake

Thana

Vihar Lake

MAINLAND OF INDIA

Madh

Versova

Aarey Dairy

Powai Lake

JAMMU AND KASHMIR

Thana Creek

PAKISTAN

TIBET

Juhu Beach

Andheri

PUNJAB

Delhi

UTTAR PRADESH

NEPAL

RAJASTHAN

BIHAR

SALSETTE

Arabian Sea

Tropic of Cancer

GUJARAT

MADHYA PRADESH

WEST BENGAL

Santa Cruz Airport

Sion Causeway

INDIA

Calcutta

ORISSA

Mahim Creek

Mt. Mary Church

Bandra

Surat

MAHARASHTRA

Sion

Trombay

BOMBAY TWIN CITY

Bombay

Poona

Mahim Bay

Deccan Plateau

Arabian Sea

Goa

ANDHRA PRADESH

Bay of Bengal

BOMBAY ISLAND

Bombay Harbour

Elephanta Island

KARNATAKA

Madras

12 miles

KERALA

Fort

TAMIL NADU

N

Colaba

SRI LANKA

government mint that lies opposite. In contrast to the grandiose bank, the Mint is a sprawling collection of modest buildings, laid out behind a classical façade that dates back to 1829. During British rule and for some years afterwards, the Mint used to stamp coins out of sheets of almost pure copper and silver. Since these metals have become truly precious, they have given way to lighter and less expensive alloys.

On the other side of Horniman Circle, away from the Mint, are the main branch offices of the leading Indian banks: the State Bank of India, the Central Bank of India, the Bank of Baroda, and so on. Equally prominent in the same area are the foreign banks, ranging from London's venerable Grindlays to the comparatively young First National City Bank of New York. More than anything else, what often distinguishes the foreign banks from the indigenous ones is the efficiency with which the former serve their customers.

Despite their best efforts, the Indian banks have failed to rival their foreign competitors in service, hemmed in as they are by an indefinably bureaucratic mentality and by involved procedures. They can take as long as an hour to cash a single cheque. No wonder, then, that their offices are often crowded with people, a sight which the uninitiated may mistake for a sign of their popularity.

There is another institution, in the centre of the financial district of the city, whose floor is usually crowded with men—in the traditional Indian dress of white *dhoti* (cotton loincloth reaching below the knee) and long shirt—carrying small notebooks and pens, and shouting and gesticulating at one another. The shouting is carried on with such passion that a casual onlooker, watching from the visitors' gallery, might well fear that a battle is about to ensue below. But nothing of the sort ever happens. The men belong to the most closely knit clan in the city, its constituents trusting one another more than they do their own blood relations. They are the members of Bombay's Stock Exchange; and it is through their violent shouts and gesticulations that these stockbrokers outbid one another in their efforts to acquire blocks of shares.

The stocks that they buy and sell cover a wide range of commodities, industries and services—from cotton, jute and tea, to mining, electricity and engineering. Many of these companies have their head offices in the Fort area. The Tatas and the Mafatlals, for example, families that own and operate two of India's three leading businesses, are rooted in Bombay. (The third family, the Birlas, has its headquarters in New Delhi.) It is from their air-conditioned, multi-storey offices in the city that the top managements of these two empires—conglomerates of companies that have widely varied interests—direct the affairs of their numerous factories and offices around the subcontinent.

Almost to a man, the stockbrokers of the Bombay market are either Gujaratis or Marwaris (people from Marwar in the state of Rajasthan); and

Central Bombay mixes skyscrapers with florid, older buildings, such as the university's Victorian tower (left) and the domed Prince of Wales Museum (right).

they and their kinsmen are the main owners of Bombay's industries and trade, whether wholesale or retail. The existence of such a bond of common origin among the leading groups of manufacturers, wholesalers and retailers can—and does—lead to certain abuses. One of the commonest is to evade the payment of excise duties and sales taxes. Often a manufacturer pays his suppliers in cash for part of the raw material he needs, then processes it unrecorded. He delivers these goods to a wholesaler, who sells them to a retailer. The latter, too, buys part of the goods in cash and the rest in the normal way. The retailer has no problem selling off the "black"—or tax-free—part of his merchandise; customers are often only too willing to forgo a formal receipt in order to escape the sales tax of perhaps 10 per cent that they are expected to pay. In this way suppliers, manufacturers and retailers all build up stocks of "black money". They can use this money either to finance further illicit operations, or such lucrative —albeit risky—projects as film-making.

The Parsis, too, are traditionally powerful in business and industry. The Tatas are Parsis, and they are undoubtedly Bombay's most famous family. Besides founding the Taj Mahal Hotel, they have helped to fund some of India's leading scientific research establishments that are to be found today in Bombay—among them, the Tata Memorial Cancer Hospital and Research Institute in the centre of the city, and the Tata Institute of Fundamental Research, founded in 1945 and moved, 17 years later, to its present site on reclaimed land at Colaba. Approached through a guarded gate and across sleek lawns, the Institute is decorated with modern sculpture and paintings, many of which were chosen by a man who was not only a Sunday painter himself but one of India's foremost scientists: Dr. Homi Bhabha. Bhabha—also a Parsi—was killed in a plane crash in Europe in 1966; but when I visited the Institute several years later, his name was still spoken of with reverence by the professors I met; and his study was preserved exactly as he had left it. Bhabha was instrumental in founding the Tata Institute and was considered the father of nuclear research in India.

In the course of my visit I met a plump and pleasant professor, Dr. D. Lal, who startled me by expressing the eccentric opinion that Hindi films— the popular, escapist fare produced in great quantities in Bombay—were the only things of interest in the city. His own scientific concern was the investigation of moon rocks; the Institute was one of only six places in the world to which NASA—the United States' National Aeronautics and Space Administration—had entrusted fragments of rocks retrieved by the U.S. astronauts in 1969. The professor took me into a large, high-security laboratory; then he opened a safe and produced the moon rocks for me to look at. They were tiny shards of dull stone that, viewed under a powerful microscope, took on the appearance of semi-precious stones, yielding up deep opaque blues and reds, and streaks and flashes of silver.

Shop signs and laundry smother a chawl (tenement) in central Bombay. Sleeping five or more to a room, chawls house three-quarters of the city's people.

At the other end of the city from the Tata Institute, where Thana Creek emerges into Bombay Harbour, is a place called Trombay. Here, in a long trough of land leading down to the irritable sea between rough hills covered with forest and flowers, a Martian landscape has been created, with huge silver domes and towers. This is the Bhabha Atomic Research Centre, inaugurated in 1957 and known as BARC. It carries out a number of projects, among them monitoring the radioactive fallout from India's nuclear establishments. The huge dome that first catches the eye as one enters, houses one of the largest reactors of its kind in the world. Within this great bubble are numerous machines, incomprehensible to me, that produce strange sounds and odours; technicians—gloved, masked and uniformed, like characters in a science-fiction film—pass one frequently in the echoing corridors. Even the flowers in the lawns between the operative areas are the product of seeds that have been subjected to experimental doses of radiation; they have large, heavy, nodding heads and unusually bright colours. The Bhabha Atomic Research Centre is the largest science establishment in the country and India's principal centre for atomic research. It was at Trombay that the first Indian nuclear explosion, which took place in 1974 in the central deserts of Rajasthan, was planned and blueprinted.

Today, the mood of the city is not what it was when I was a child in the 1940s. It is a neurotic place, like most other large cities, and its expanse is no longer so much one of leisurely sprawl as of crowded clutter. Since so many old houses have been pulled down and replaced by skyscrapers, the

The entrance to the Great Cave on the island of Elephanta in Bombay Harbour provides an august setting for a picnic held by a British party in the 1870s. The several chambers of the cave were hewn out of solid rock, possibly as early as the 6th Century A.D., to serve as Hindu shrines. They contain numerous reliefs, notably a giant bust of the Hindu god Shiva (right), portrayed with three heads to express three different aspects assumed by the deity.

whole face of Bombay seems to have tightened into a scowl, streaked in the monsoon season with rain.

The monsoons usually arrive in early June, when the first huge storm clouds drift up from the sea. They depart in September—often after one final, wistful explosion of the clouds—having cascaded an average of 66 inches of rain over their four months' duration. During the monsoon season the city may also be hit by tropical cyclones, though fortunately these wind storms are a rare occurrence. If they blow in from the Arabian Sea, the consequences are serious; but if they originate in the Bay of Bengal, they are rather weary from lengthy overland travel by the time they reach the city; moreover they have already collided with the Ghats, the hill complex on the mainland east of Bombay. These milder storms can sometimes even be rather beneficent, if they come at a time when the heavy rains can do good to the crops in the city's hinterland, rather than simply flatten them by their force.

In spite of the seasonal deluges, the city suffers from chronic water shortages. The two islands on which it is built ensure that the catchment area is strictly circumscribed; and although there are large lakes on Salsette that are used as reservoirs, they rely entirely on rain-water to replenish them, without the aid of rivers or springs. Should the rains be slighter than usual in any year, the effect is felt immediately in a city whose industrial and domestic demands continue to grow steadily—and where water rationing is an accepted fact of life.

The city's oppressive summer temperature cools down a little during the monsoon season; but the coolest time of year comes during the months which in Europe would be taken to be winter: that is to say, from December to about March. Even so, constant evaporation from the sea and the creeks makes for a densely humid atmosphere all the year round. The mean annual temperature in Bombay is in the vicinity of 80°F. The month of May is a damp furnace, with temperatures of up to 95°F, only relieved by the arrival of the first rains.

The heat and humidity are made even more unpleasant by the exhaust fumes from the city's throbbing traffic. The last time I was in Bombay, the traffic was wilder than I had ever seen it before, in spite of the fact that only 2 per cent of Bombay's population own private cars. The traffic police in their blue and yellow turbans and uniforms seemed helpless against the onrushing surf of motor vehicles that swerve from one side of the road to the other, avoiding—and sometimes failing to avoid—collisions with buses, bicycles, buffaloes and people.

Once, after a particularly narrow escape in a taxi driven by a Muslim, I took it upon myself to utter a mild rebuke. He turned his head to reply and nearly ran into the pavement. "Sahib," he said with a grin, "Allah destined the day of my birth. He also destined the day of my death. If it is today, so let it be." Unfortunately, this attitude seems to be shared by

A dhow, the type of fishing and trading boat that has plied the Arabian Sea and the Indian Ocean for at least 500 years, sails past the dome of an experimental nuclear reactor at the Bhabha Atomic Research Centre. Inaugurated in 1957, the Centre is situated at Trombay on the northern shore of Bombay Harbour.

pedestrians of every creed, who sometimes wander down the middle of the road while the traffic around them behaves like dodgem cars at a fair.

The same devil-may-care attitude is shown by those who, unable to force their way inside the incredibly crowded trains at commuter hours, stand on the footboards or cling to the doors and windows. The resulting fatalities are not so much indications of a paucity of trains as of a plenitude of people, whose presence inevitably affects the quality of almost every aspect of daily life in the city.

The buses, too, red double-deckers of the sort familiar to Londoners, frequently carry more passengers than they were built for. One result is that, on both trains and buses, the Bombay male can indulge in a favoured pastime known in India as "Eve-teasing": that is to say, fondling and ogling the prettier women in the crowd. The same opportunity is also seized on the pavements, which in the centre of the city are usually so full of people that one sometimes literally has to force a passage through.

One aspect of life in Bombay that has not changed since my youth—or indeed, in all likelihood, since the days of the Kolis—is the mass production of that curious delicacy, Bombay Duck, which has long been responsible for one element in the city's characteristic multiple smell. Bombay Duck is the name given to the lean, silver *bombil* fish after it has been dried in the sun and reduced to a hard, brown, brittle sliver widely encountered these days as a restaurant snack. For the Kolis, it was part of their staple diet. The fish are still hung out to dry in the Koli villages along the coast and even in central Bombay, where some of the fishermen land their catches at a site adjoining Colaba's Sassoon Dock.

I can remember when the newspaper office where my father worked was close to this waterfront. He would soak his handkerchief in eau-de-Cologne before he was driven off to work each morning so that, on his arrival, he could hold it to his nostrils for the few short steps it took him to walk from the car to the lift and be whisked up to his air-conditioned editorial chamber, which was not only sound-proof but smell-proof. There his secretary maintained another stock of eau-de-Cologne, which he used similarly when he left the office. My father had been a war correspondent and had sniffed the reek of battlefields in China, Burma and Korea; but the stench of Bombay Duck in the making was evidently far worse. Still, the malodorous process was apparently worthwhile; for I must admit that whenever he was offered Bombay Duck as a relish at dinner, he accepted it avidly.

There are, of course, other, more delicate reminders of the Bombay I once knew—and of the Bombay that existed long before that. Whatever my divided feelings about the city where I was born, I carry with me, always, pleasant memories of its beauty. Wherever I can still glimpse the impressions of all that first defined this great city for me amid the noisy, go-ahead, modern metropolis, they surprise me: an old house, half hidden by flowering trees; the vivid blue of the Arabian Sea lisping against the sea wall of Marine Drive; the Queen's Necklace lighting the curve of the bay after dusk; or a barefooted Koli woman, the sand under her feet and a basket of dripping fish on her head, looking out to sea as her ancestors must have done when they were the only inhabitants of the islands—before the tall western ships came up from the horizon, with the sunset reflected like blood on their sails.

Fisherfolk of Versova

Under the painted eye on his boat, a Versova fisherman brings a prize specimen ashore. The woman wears her sari Koli-style, twisted between her legs.

Along the 40-mile stretch of Bombay's Arabian Sea coast are a handful of villages occupied by the Kolis, a people whose ancestors first settled in the area about 2,000 years ago. Now, as in ancient times, the Kolis live by fishing the inshore waters from their small wooden boats, then selling their catch in the city, either dried—like *bombil*, known in English as Bombay Duck—or else fresh. Inevitably, however, the Kolis' traditional way of life is altering: government loans encourage them to modernize their methods, and city jobs are luring away their better-educated youths. And yet the Kolis retain their special identity, speaking their own dialect and observing their own customs—from religious rites to everyday dress styles. Today, the highest concentration of Kolis—a community of several thousand—is at Versova, 15 miles north of central Bombay.

Villagers sort the day's catch. Once, most of it was sold dried; now ice is available locally for packing and more can be taken fresh to Bombay's markets.

Koli women, here gathered in a Versova market, traditionally handle every process after the catch is landed, from gutting and trimming to drying and selling.

Working on the slab of her market-stall, a woman splits the backbone of a large marsa (jew-fish), many of which weigh as much as 35 pounds.

A Versova woman naps among drying fish. Small species need only a few hours in the sun; the larger bombil are hung on frames to catch both sun and wind.

In an unchanged corner of Versova, a family gathers on the doorstep. Traditional cane-and-mud huts are giving way to brick-and-concrete houses (background).

2

The Imprint of Empire

As I first remember Bombay during the Second World War, it was still a British city in many obvious ways. It was ruled by a British governor and administered by a civil service that the British had set up. My parents and I lived in one of the more British parts of the city. We had a flat on the west side of the Oval, above which floated barrage balloons, tethered to the turf by lengthy cables. These gyrating giants, a precaution against low-level Japanese air attack, were the symbols of the British war in which Bombay had become embroiled. On the eastern side of the park were the Victorian Gothic civic buildings that were erected in the 1860s and 1870s: the immense, pinnacled High Court—red tiles above dark basalt; the university library with its yellow sandstone clock-tower, flanked by the university Convocation Hall, with turrets at its four corners; and the old Secretariat, containing the offices of civil servants. Beyond this serried assembly, as yet unchallenged on the skyline, lay the heart of the city: the prosperous shops and offices around Flora Fountain; and beyond these, the wide swathe of the harbour.

If you came out of our apartment block and turned left, you arrived after a short walk at the wrinkled yellow edifice of Churchgate Station, from which commuting office workers in white shirts and trousers hurried each morning and to which they returned in the evening, to be swallowed up in its smoky mouth until the following day. Outside the railway station there were ranks of what were called *ghoda-ghadis*—gaudily painted carriages pulled by bony horses festooned with rosettes and desultory flowers. These vehicles served people working at a distance from the station; but after the morning rush and before the evening turmoil they often took the children of more affluent families for sightseeing rides.

The carriages smelt of both horse and driver, since the drivers normally used them as their bedrooms. There was also the odour of hay and other fodder, and the seat coverings were usually split. But amidst the creak of leather and wheels a child could enjoy himself for half an hour or so, watching the city slowly unfold. A hundred years earlier the British, too, had liked to promenade in the evenings in horse-drawn carriages, going south, like us, to Colaba and back. We trotted down Marine Drive, the Arabian Sea spewing foam beyond the sea wall, then along the reclaimed areas of Back Bay and down Cuffe Parade—once called the Esplanade. The horse, swivelling in its shafts, would then lead homeward along Queen's Road towards Churchgate, passing the Cooperage—an open space, named after a barrel-makers' shed, that was now the site of a small football

Outside Victoria Terminus, one of Bombay's three central railway stations, a British lion receives its annual cleaning. Many memorials to the British Raj have disappeared since India gained her independence in 1947, but this lion —one of a pair guarding the station entrance— remains as an imposing reminder of almost three centuries of British rule in Bombay.

stadium. Then came the Bandstand, where on certain afternoons a uniformed band performed and where every evening there were scruffy ponies that children could ride, their *ayahs* trotting anxiously behind.

In those days the population of Bombay was still much the same —around the million mark—as it had been when King George V and Queen Mary passed through the city on their state visit in 1911. Although the industrial districts were as congested and squalid as they are today, there was little obvious sign of overcrowding in the central avenues and parks, where statues of the Queen-Empress Victoria, the King-Emperor Edward VII and various proconsuls looked down from lofty plinths. Many more streets than now were lined with trees; and although one could not say that Bombay was, by Western standards, an especially hygienic city, the atmosphere—at least—was spacious; there seemed to be a logic about the place, as though things fitted where they were meant to.

Not only the appearance and feel of the city but the life we led made me think that Bombay was British. My parents were Christians (Catholics). Neither spoke an Indian language nor, indeed, any other language apart from English; they did not consider it necessary. Both practised professions in a manner brought to India by the British. My father had been to Oxford to read history; then he went to Lincoln's Inn in London, to study law. On his return to India he first worked, not very profitably, as a barrister, then decided he should write for his supper; and in 1936 he joined *The Times of India*, the great British paper founded as the *Bombay Times* in 1838, whose editorship generally carried a knighthood with it. My mother, whose own mother, Dr. Cecilia D'Monte, was the first Indian woman doctor, had been trained in Bombay as a pathologist and she worked at the large Cama Hospital in the centre of the city. In those days not many

In a scene dating from the 1880s, a flotilla of steamships, sailing vessels and small craft ride at anchor off the pier known as Apollo Bunder where passengers from Britain disembarked from ships of the P. & O. Line. Following the opening of the Suez Canal in 1869, the trip from England took a mere three weeks instead of the three months or more required previously, when ships had to journey round the Cape.

wives, whether Indian or British, worked. But Bombay had reached a period of change, partly because of the influence of Indian nationalism, which sought a degree of emancipation for women, and partly through the socialist beliefs that were held by most young British intellectuals in the 1930s. The first influence had a direct impact on all Indians, the second upon the British in India and through them upon the lives of Westernized Indians such as ourselves.

My father played some part in the changes of the 1940s. He became not only the first Indian to be appointed a senior editor of *The Times of India* but also the first Indian to be appointed as a war correspondent: he was posted to the Burma and China theatres. Before this, it had been thought unwise to send out Indian journalists as war correspondents lest they report British reverses with too much fervour. My father came back from the front having mixed with other correspondents of many nationalities. He had met many young British officers who had no consciousness of colour and no desire for India to remain a British colony. He also talked regularly with Indian nationalists. He soon decided that there was a great need to change the power structure of the paper he worked for.

He chose a very down-to-earth way to do this. Each of the British editors of *The Times of India* had a key to the executive lavatory and used a special cafeteria. Senior Indian editors (and there were only two: my father and another young Oxford-educated man, D. F. Karaka) were denied these privileges. Most of the British staff were friends of Karaka and of my father, more so indeed than they were of Francis Low, the dour Scotsman who edited the paper. My father demanded that the senior Indian staff be accorded the same perks as the British and eventually, in 1942, Low bowed before the combined wills of my father and of his enlightened young British colleagues. From then on, the editorial staff of *The Times of India*, both Indian and British, worked together as professional and racial equals. In 1950 my father became Editor.

Our home life was, I suppose, fairly typical of Westernized Indians, who were mostly Parsis and Christians, and also of ordinary British families. The food we ate was mainly British: roast mutton or beef, chops or steaks, followed by an awful pudding or by ice cream. We had several servants, who lived in: a bearer, or butler, who served food and drink; the *ayah*; the cook; two *hamals*—cleaners who swept and dusted; and our chauffeur, who slept by the car. A sweeper, the lowest category of Indian domestic servant, came in daily to clean the lavatories.

My mother shopped mainly in three places. Two were off Flora Fountain: the gigantic Army and Navy Stores, providing tinned food, clothes, home furnishings and, at seasonal times, Easter eggs and Christmas trees; and Pyrke's Provision Stores, which supplied items such as eggs, ham and bacon. The third place was Crawford Market, which was divided into sections for fruit and vegetables, fresh fish and meat. It was, and still is, an enormous structure of discoloured grey cement and stone wearing an untidy hat of corrugated iron. Its chief distinction, apart from its size, is a series of bas-reliefs designed by J. Lockwood Kipling, whose son Rudyard, born in Bombay in 1865, later won for himself a reputation as the leading poet of empire.

Once or twice a month there would be a party in our house. Sometimes the guests were British civilians and rich Indians—mostly Parsis in shipping and industry. On these occasions evening dress was worn. At less formal parties young British officers and Indian nationalists came. A frequent guest at these parties was D. G. Tendulkar, a small man wearing a coarse shirt and shorts he had woven himself. Tendulkar had been a Communist and had spent part of the 1920s in Russia. Later he had gone to Germany and, when the Nazis started to flex their muscles, he was interned in a concentration camp and had all his teeth knocked out. On his release and return to India in the late 1930s he became a follower of Mahatma Gandhi, under whose leadership India achieved independence.

When I first knew Tendulkar, he was writing an eight-volume official biography of the Mahatma (it was published between 1951 and 1954). He took me in hand and showed me how other people lived in Bombay. I used to visit him in the slum where he had his home, in the district of Kalbadevi, near Crawford Market. To reach his room—which was tidy in an almost fanatical way and filled with books, delicate Chinese ivories and Indian bronzes—I had to climb a stained staircase upon which people slept in the attitudes of the dead. Tendulkar would feed me with what he ate himself—literally a handful of rice and lentils—and conducted me on walks through the industrial area of the city. There the chimneys of the cotton mills belched acrid smoke, and crowds of ragged workers surged in and out of the gates when the whistles sounded the change of shifts.

Another of my father's friends was an English publisher, Roy Hawkins, known to my father as "Hawk". He had come to India as a very young man in the early 1930s to work for the local office of the Oxford University Press. At first he had lived in what was called a "chummery": a large house occupied by a number of young English bachelors who shared the rent and the cost of food and servants. Later Hawk moved into a bungalow of his own, surrounded by flowering trees and shrubs, on Cumballa Hill. Hawk adhered closely to the pattern that intellectuals of the time were supposed to follow: he talked through a pipe that was forever clenched in his mouth; he played chess; he went for long healthy walks into wooded hills around the city; and he was interested in a broad range of cultural activities. Hawk, my father and a group of other like-minded people were instrumental in founding the Silverfish Club. This institution, which had a lending library and a bar, also offered its members lectures on literature.

The familiars of the Silverfish were often members also of the Royal Asiatic Society, another haven of clubby British culture in Bombay. The

An elderly chowkidar, a watchman or caretaker employed by such concerns as public offices, banks and factories, enjoys an off-duty moment beside a refreshment stall. His military bearing and khaki uniform—complete with puttees, the protective cotton leggings first worn by the Indian Army in the late 19th Century—reflect the enduring influence of the British in Bombay.

Society's library, founded in 1804, was on the first floor of the porticoed Town Hall at Horniman Circle, near the harbour, and I often visited it with my father. To reach it, you had to climb a marble staircase flanked by statues of former governors of Bombay; then amidst decrepit shelves that smelt of rotten leather and old paper, we delved for our books. As I recollect, the library had one of the most important collections of first editions in the world, badly kept though they were. When we had unearthed what we wanted, a uniformed servant would carry the books to the car.

The Royal Asiatic Society was only one of the many institutions that had laid a civilized framework for cultural life, law and public administration in Bombay. By the time the city reached its late-Victorian apogee, bedecked in municipal Gothic and prosperous from its harbour trade and the products of its smoking factories, the British could refer to it as *urbs prima in Indis*, the greatest city in the East.

There was little in the early history of Bombay to suggest that one day it would rise to such pre-eminence. In the early 17th Century it was a small Portuguese settlement with a rather second-rate fort. When King Charles II received Bombay in his bride's dowry, he also got Tangier and a lump sum of £500,000. Clearly Bombay was something of a make-weight in this package. The King and his ministers were remarkably ill-informed about their new acquisition. One of the negotiators of Charles's marriage treaty—the British Lord Chancellor, the Earl of Clarendon—described the new addition to the British realm as "an island with the towns, and castles therein, which are within a very little distance of Brazil".

By 1668 the Crown was happy to lease Bombay to the East India Company for £10 a year. The Company could best be described as a confederation of adventurous London merchants. On its formation in 1600 it had obtained from Queen Elizabeth I a charter giving it the exclusive right to bring goods from the East into England. When it acquired Bombay the Company already had "factories" (trading stations) in India, notably at Surat, 150 miles north of Bombay, and at Madras and Hooghly (near what was to be Calcutta) on the east coast. It had established these stations after negotiations with the Indian rulers upon whose uncertain favour it depended. Most of the subcontinent was then part of the Mughal Empire, a Muslim dominion founded in 1526 by the central Asian prince, Babar, descendant of the Mongol conqueror Tamerlane. Under the Emperor of the time, Aurangzeb, the Mughals had expanded their empire to its greatest extent, but they were finding it increasingly difficult to control certain provinces, especially Gujarat and surrounding areas in the west.

Gujarat's chief port was Surat, admirably situated both for India's inland markets and the ancient sea routes to the Persian Gulf and east Africa. The Portuguese and Dutch also had trading posts at Surat and here the East India Company had established its headquarters for western India—under

whose jurisdiction Bombay was now placed. Surat, like Madras and later Calcutta, was governed by a President and Council, and was styled a Presidency. Eventually, when British power became predominant in India, the three East India Company Presidencies were to encompass not only ports but vast areas of hinterland in the north-east, west and south-east.

From the first, the East India Company enjoyed full sovereignty over Bombay, including the right to maintain a military garrison, levy taxes and administer justice. But apart from this, Bombay seemed to have little to recommend it. Contrary to what Lord Clarendon had reported, Bombay had no towns. The population of about 10,000, made up mostly of Indian fishing communities but including also some half-castes and Portuguese soldiers, traders and priests, lived in villages and a few houses scattered among dense plantations of coconut palms and other fruit-bearing trees. Large parts of the island were submerged at high tide. Small boats traded desultorily up and down the coast in coconuts, salt fish and copra, but conditions were hardly ideal for profitable trade. The deep inlets along the coastline provided refuge for marauding pirates, and access to inland markets was blocked by the mountains of the Western Ghats, a towering blue rampart clearly visible to the east. In the hinterland beyond were the fierce Maratha armies who, under their leader Shivaji, had already conquered large stretches of the Deccan, the great inland plateau of central India, and now prowled around looking for other territories to devour.

However, more dangerous to Englishmen than any Maratha horsemen or pirates was the climate of Bombay and its swamps. The island stank, partly because the palm trees shut out the sea breezes and partly because the local Kolis fertilized their coconut groves by heaping decaying fish around the trees. The rotting debris contaminated the drinking wells. "And in the Morning," recorded an early visitor, "there is generally seen a thick Fog among those trees that affects both the Brains and Lungs of Europeans and breeds Consumptions, Fevers and Fluxes." In modern terminology, the chief diseases were malaria, scurvy, smallpox and cholera, and also bubonic plague, which ravaged the islands in the last two decades of the 17th Century. When a clergyman, John Ovington, arrived in 1689, he was horrified by the state of the British community and wrote back to London that Bombay was "nought but a charnel house". According to a proverb prevalent among the settlers, it was a place "in which two Mussouns [monsoons] are the Age of a Man": if a new arrival survived longer than two years he was lucky.

The English made matters worse for themselves by starting their day with seven-course breakfasts washed down with claret, and by wearing thick woollen garments even in the heat of summer. The islands offered little opportunity for recreation. Trade was slack and there was not much money to be made in government or military service. It was hardly surprising that the first settlers, believing themselves to be a legion of the

Seven Stepping-Stones to a City

A.D.	
c. 1st Century	Koli fishermen settle on the future site of Bombay: a cluster of seven small islands later named Worli, Mahim, Parel-Sion, Mazagaon, Mumbadevi, Old Woman's Island and Colaba
c. 200	Buddhists occupy cave temple complex at Kanheri, on Salsette Island, immediately north of Bombay
c. 550	Hindu craftsmen carve their first massive sculptures and reliefs in excavated caves on Elephanta Island
c. 1050	Walkeshwar Hindu temple complex built near Malabar Point on Mumbadevi Island
1294	Hindu king, Bhimadeva, also known as Bimba, in retreat from Muslim raids into western India, founds a settlement on Mahim Island
1297	Muslims occupy Gujarat, mainland area north of Bombay
1401	Bombay's islands come under rule of the Sultans of Gujarat
1498	Portuguese explorer Vasco da Gama lands in south-west India, after pioneering sea route from Europe
1509	Portuguese forces defeat an allied Indian fleet off coast of Gujarat. Portuguese dominate Indian Ocean until arrival of Dutch and English in 17th Century
1526-28	Mughals—Muslims of Mongolian origin—invade India and establish an empire with capital in Delhi
1534	Sultan of Gujarat cedes port of Bassein, along with Bombay islands and Salsette, to the Portuguese
1613	Mughal Emperor Jehangir allows English to trade at Surat, 160 miles north of Bombay. East India Company, a consortium of London merchants, establishes its western India headquarters there
1640-80	Local leader Shivaji establishes Hindu kingdom of Maharashtra in Bombay's hinterland
1661	Portugal cedes Bombay to England as part of the dowry of Catharine of Braganza, on her marriage to King Charles II. But the Portuguese Viceroy at Goa prevents the British Governor from taking possession
1665	Humphrey Cooke, second British Governor, occupies Bombay. Population is about 10,000, consisting of Kolis, Bhandaris, Portuguese and half-castes
1668	Charles II leases Bombay to the East India Company
1669-77	Governor Gerald Aungier improves Bombay's fortifications and initiates land reclamation to unite five northernmost islands. He organizes militia and police, and by proclaiming religious neutrality attracts Indian settlers from surrounding districts
1687	East India Company transfers western headquarters from Surat to strategically safer Bombay
1713-60	Marathas (inhabitants of kingdom of Maharashtra) consolidate their power into a Confederacy led by a succession of chief ministers, or Peshwas
1718	Anglican Church of St. Thomas completed
1728	City's western sea wall, protecting low-lying interior from inundation at high tide, completed
1736	At British invitation, Lavji Naserwanji Wadia, Parsi master-carpenter in shipyards at Surat, moves his business to Bombay
1738	Marathas capture Bassein and Salsette from Portuguese, and go on to achieve control of Gujarat
1744	City's population reaches an estimated 70,000
1775-82	British in India embark on the first of three campaigns against the Marathas; they gain possession of Salsette
1780-1800	Political unrest, and silting of harbour, bring about decline of the trading post of Surat, causing migration of merchants—mainly Parsis—to Bombay. Cotton and opium trade develop with China
1803	Three-day fire destroys three-quarters of city's Fort area, permitting co-ordinated rebuilding. Causeway built to link Bombay with Salsette
1803-5	Marathas suffer defeat in Second Maratha War
1817-18	After Third Maratha War, British annex Maratha territories in western India, forming a much enlarged Bombay Presidency
1819-27	Governor Mountstuart Elphinstone builds schools and carries out important social and legal reforms

damned, behaved as such. They fought among themselves. They also cohabited with the Koli fisherwomen—an entertainment they called "black velvet"—so adding to the half-caste community. In 1668 the directors of the East India Company started to despatch "sober and civil" single women from England in an attempt to increase the European population, but not many unwithered English roses can have found their way to Bombay; soon reports were circulating that the newcomers were also behaving in a way "scandalous to our nation, religion and government interest". Orders were given that unless their behaviour improved they should be confined "and fed with bread and water, till they are embarqued . . . for England". One has no idea whether they were.

The first British official shrewd enough to see that Bombay had positive qualities was Gerald Aungier, who in 1669 became the East India Company's President at Surat and therefore Governor of Bombay. He saw that Bombay, being an island, could be more easily defended than Surat; indeed, with the right fortifications and armaments, it could be made virtually impregnable from land and sea. The great scimitar-shaped harbour offered possibilities too: Aungier described Bombay's harbour as "certainly the fairest, largest and securest in all these parts of India, where a hundred sail of tall ships may ride all the year safe with good moorage".

Aungier realized that, if Bombay were to thrive, it had to attract a working population. He therefore set about enticing merchants and craftsmen from the mainland to settle in Bombay. At the south-east corner of the island a substantial town began to grow around the old fort left by the Portuguese. Services on the quayside were improved. An English judge was installed and a court-house set up in the most frequented part of the town's bazaar. A militia was formed, a police force organized and a mint established. Most important, Aungier offered immigrants religious freedom and allowed them to follow their own customs without interference—something that had been denied under Portuguese rule, as it still was by neighbouring Indian princes. Attracted by these advantages, merchants and bankers came from adjacent territories to settle in Bombay. By the time Aungier died in 1677, the predominantly Indian population of Bombay had risen to 60,000. Meanwhile, Surat was becoming untenable, partly because the Mughal tax-gatherers were making extortionate demands in their efforts to finance Aurangzeb's interminable wars; and partly because of the threat of the Marathas, who had sacked the town in 1664 and again in 1670. In 1687 Bombay succeeded Surat as headquarters of the western Presidency.

Bombay quickly displayed cosmopolitan qualities that were to mark it off from other Indian cities. There was no sharp distinction between "White Town" and "Black Town", as in Madras, for example; here the Indians lived clustered around the British in the centre of town. Later the British, while retaining their town houses and offices, built garden houses in the

On January 10, 1912, after their triumphant five-week state visit to India, King George V and Queen Mary (below) descend the landing-steps of Apollo Bunder to be taken back to the imperial yacht. The farewell ceremony (inset) was held in front of a magnificent plaster arch, specially erected for the visit. The arch was replaced in 1924 by the present Gateway of India.

pleasant suburbs of Byculla, Parel, Mazagaon and Malabar Hill—and the more prosperous Indians followed them.

Among those wealthier Indians were the Parsis. The British had first encountered the Parsis in Surat, and had found them valuable as middle men between themselves and their Indian suppliers. Unlike the Hindus or the Muslims, the Parsis had no dietetic or caste laws to inhibit social intercourse with the British, and they possessed skills that the British needed: they were traders and shipbuilders. They soon became the most influential group in Bombay. In 1735 the East India Company, finding it difficult to procure enough ships and repair them locally, persuaded a Parsi shipbuilder, Lavji Naserwanji Wadia, to move his operations from Surat to Bombay. He arrived in 1736, bought in teak from the mainland and established a shipyard. From then on the Wadia family was to be inextricably linked with the history of the Bombay docks. Other Parsis came, still acting as middle men, and some undertook longer journeys—to China for example—that were forbidden to Hindus by their religious code.

For most of the 18th Century, the services rendered by the harbour and dockyards to the East India Company's fleet were all that kept Bombay from being run down to a provincial outstation. Trade continued to be unprofitable, and Mughal and Maratha governments remained in power on the nearby mainland. Unlike the two other principal British bases at Madras and Calcutta, Bombay thus had no opportunity to acquire territory and gain revenue from land taxes and tribute money. The men sent there from Britain tended to be distant relatives of the less influential of the Company's directors; and even by the end of the century the British settlers at Bombay numbered less than a thousand, including seamen and soldiers.

However, as the 18th Century drew to a close, new advantages in maintaining a strong Bombay became clear. The British government in London, fighting a global war against the French and their Revolution, saw the settlement as a valuable military base and encouraged the East India Company to keep ploughing resources into it. At the same time, trade was showing the first signs of picking up. Among Bombay's traditional exports had been handmade, cotton piece-goods, shipped in small quantities to many destinations. But now Bombay merchants were beginning to export raw cotton to China from the great cotton-growing districts of Gujarat, and to this was soon added another export also destined for China: opium from the Malwa district of central India.

These merchants worked, not for the East India Company, but for private British and Indian firms, particularly those owned by Parsi merchant princes, who began moving from Surat to Bombay again in larger numbers than ever during the 1780s and 1790s. The Bombay dockyards, owned entirely by Parsis, began to step up the construction of large ships designed to carry the cargoes of bulky cotton to Canton, the chief port of destination. The Parsis became even richer and more powerful. As one modern

historian has put it, "the Parsi shipbuilder rather than the English merchant was the true maker of Bombay".

In the 19th Century Bombay finally became a great city. From being a port and dockyard, fortified against attack from land and sea, it developed into an industrial, commercial and administrative hub of empire, linked by road and rail to the interior of India and by new sea routes to Britain. British naval patrols had practically halted piracy along the coast and the only remaining threat was the Maratha ascendancy on the mainland.

In the north, Maratha power was restrained by that of the Mughals; but in west and central India the Maratha Confederacy, formed by the agreement of various leaders around 1730, was unchallenged. Foremost among these leaders was the Peshwa, who governed the Confederacy from Poona, in the mountains 75 miles from Bombay. Since the formation of the Confederacy, successive Peshwas had signed treaties with the British; but these were short-lived and three major wars were fought between British and Maratha armies in the late 18th and early 19th Centuries.

The First Maratha War ended in 1782 with the cession to the British of Salsette Island. By that time the ambitions of the Peshwas in northern India had been upset by the Afghans in a great battle near Delhi in 1761. From the 1790s, the strength of the Peshwas was further undermined by dissension within the Confederacy. They hated each other even more than they did the foreigners and, in India's disunity, the British saw their chance. In 1803, during the Second Maratha War, General Sir Arthur Wellesley, the future Duke of Wellington and victor of Waterloo, destroyed the flower of the Maratha armies in two decisive battles, and thereafter the British Resident (that is, ambassador) installed at the Peshwa's court at Poona increasingly interfered in domestic Maratha policy. In the last Maratha War, the Peshwa made a desperate but futile bid to throw off British tutelage and, in 1818, the East India Company annexed his territories in western Maharashtra. These lands, added to select districts already acquired in Gujarat, transformed the western Presidency into a province of 70,000 square miles with a 400-mile coastline stretching from Surat to Goa. Bombay at last had a hinterland.

Over the next 40 years, in a series of pioneering projects, British engineers and Indian labourers opened up this great region to transport. In 1830 a new road was completed from Bombay to Poona; other roads pushed northwards. India's first railway came into service in 1853, running 23 miles from Bombay to Thana. It subsequently became the Great Indian Peninsular Railway, which by 1871 bound Bombay to central and northern India. The most impressive part of the new line was the Bhor Ghat incline, leading up through the Western Ghats. Opened in 1863, it reached, in one long gradient of fifteen and a half miles, a height of 1,832 feet. Gone were the days when packs of bullocks had carried goods up and down the mountains by road, or when travellers had to get out of carts and palanquins to walk the steepest part of the ascent. The old journey had taken at least 24 hours; by rail the time was cut to six hours and the cost drastically reduced. The Bombay, Baroda and Central India Railway, opened in 1860, provided a similarly fast and economical service to Gujarat.

While Bombay's ties with the mainland of India were being strengthened, changes in shipping routes benefited the port. In the 17th and 18th Centuries, Bombay had not usually been a first port of call in India; ships struggling around the Cape of Good Hope were more likely to head for Madras or Calcutta, a voyage of up to six months. But in 1830 a much faster route was pioneered. Travellers came by ship through the Mediterranean to Alexandria, then overland via Cairo to Suez (first by camel, later by rail) and continued by ship once more through the Red Sea to Bombay.

The Suez overland route was uncomfortable for passengers, but it took only 30 days. The opening of the Suez Canal in 1869 reduced this time to three weeks or less and Bombay became the major port for passengers arriving in India, mainly civil servants and army officers on their way to posts all over the subcontinent. Bombay also became the main entrepôt for the import of manufactured goods and the export of Indian primary products—mainly cotton, wheat and oilseeds.

It seems extraordinary how the fortunes of one country are often based upon those of another, perhaps without either people knowing what the other country looks like. The wealth of the city of Bombay was based largely upon changes in the demand for cotton in the West. During the early

Dynasts of Trade

The fortunes of the Tata family—members of Bombay's influential Parsi community—were founded in the late 19th Century by Jamsetjee Tata, a formidable entrepreneur whose business concerns have grown into the largest private group of companies in India. Born in 1839, Jamsetjee began by establishing highly profitable cotton mills in Bombay; with the profits that he amassed he built a magnificent mansion, Esplanade House (right), on Waudby Road in the city centre; and he set up a number of philanthropic enterprises before his death in 1904. His vision of a thriving India rested on the belief that political independence was meaningless without economic self-sufficiency.

Numerous objets d'art and pieces of European furniture pack a sitting room in Esplanade House.

In the Spanish-style central courtyard of Esplanade House, Jamsetjee used to tend his exotic plants.

Like a true Victorian patriarch, the pioneer industrialist Jamsetjee Tata (right) sits at the centre of a formal family group in 1897 comprising his wife, sons and daughters-in-law. The whole family resided in Esplanade House, designed by the British architect J. Morris to Jamsetjee's own specifications.

19th Century, the owners of the new steam-powered cotton mills of northern England had a growing need for raw cotton at a time when they were paying higher and higher prices for the long-stapled variety grown in the southern, slave-owning states of newly independent America. The short-stapled cotton of Gujarat was more difficult to work with, but it was cheap; and so millions of bales, stinking and spotted with the black seeds of the cotton plants, began to pass through Bombay's docks on their way to Liverpool and Manchester. When the American Civil War broke out over the issue of slavery in 1861, American cotton supplies were cut off and Bombay's own exports doubled. Between then and 1865 more than £81 million was paid to Bombay merchants by Manchester mill-owners.

But there had always been something paradoxical about Bombay's cotton trade with England. Raw cotton from Gujarat was shipped to Lancashire, spun and woven into cloth and brought back to Bombay—a round trip of 20,000 miles. The Lancashire cloth provided cheap garments for Indian peasants, among them Gujarati cotton-pickers; but it also undermined the Indian handloom industry. It occurred to certain enterprising Indian merchants that, since India supplied both the raw material and the market, cotton mills should be built locally too.

From the mid-19th Century this was done: much of the money that Bombay's merchants earned from cotton exports was ploughed back by them into the construction of mills, and thousands of Indians were initiated into the mysteries of shift work. As Tendulkar put it to me, brown men were enslaved because of the efforts, in another part of the world, to make black men free. A Parsi, C. N. Davar, raised the capital to open Bombay's first steam-powered cotton mill in 1854. All kinds of problems had to be solved. Equipment and skilled mechanics to install it had to be brought from England; and, in those days, few local people could be trusted to handle complex machinery. But these difficulties were overcome and, by 1860, six more Parsi-owned mills were in operation. A local newspaper proudly boasted that: "Bombay has long been the Liverpool of the East and she is now become the Manchester also." By the turn of the century, there were more than 80 cotton mills in the city.

Ever since Bombay had won its own hinterland from the Marathas in 1818, it had been developing, not just as a maritime and industrial city, but also as a military, educational and administrative centre. All the main schools, government offices and barracks, and the highest courts of law in the Presidency were built there. Alongside the merchant princes of Bombay—the shipbuilders, the bankers and businessmen—emerged a thriving intelligentsia that gave a new impetus to political and cultural life.

The Honourable Mountstuart Elphinstone, a pragmatic and far-sighted Scot who became Governor of Bombay in 1819, had lent his authority to the notion that Indians should have the benefit of an English education

During outbreaks of bubonic plague that caused some 114,000 deaths in Bombay between 1896 and 1899, the British authorities adopted harsh measures to stop the pestilence spreading. Water from flushing-engines (top) was aimed squarely into homes, while lime solution was applied by hand (below) to the outside walls. The high-handed treatment of bewildered Indians outraged all sections of the community, and even led to the killing of two British officials.

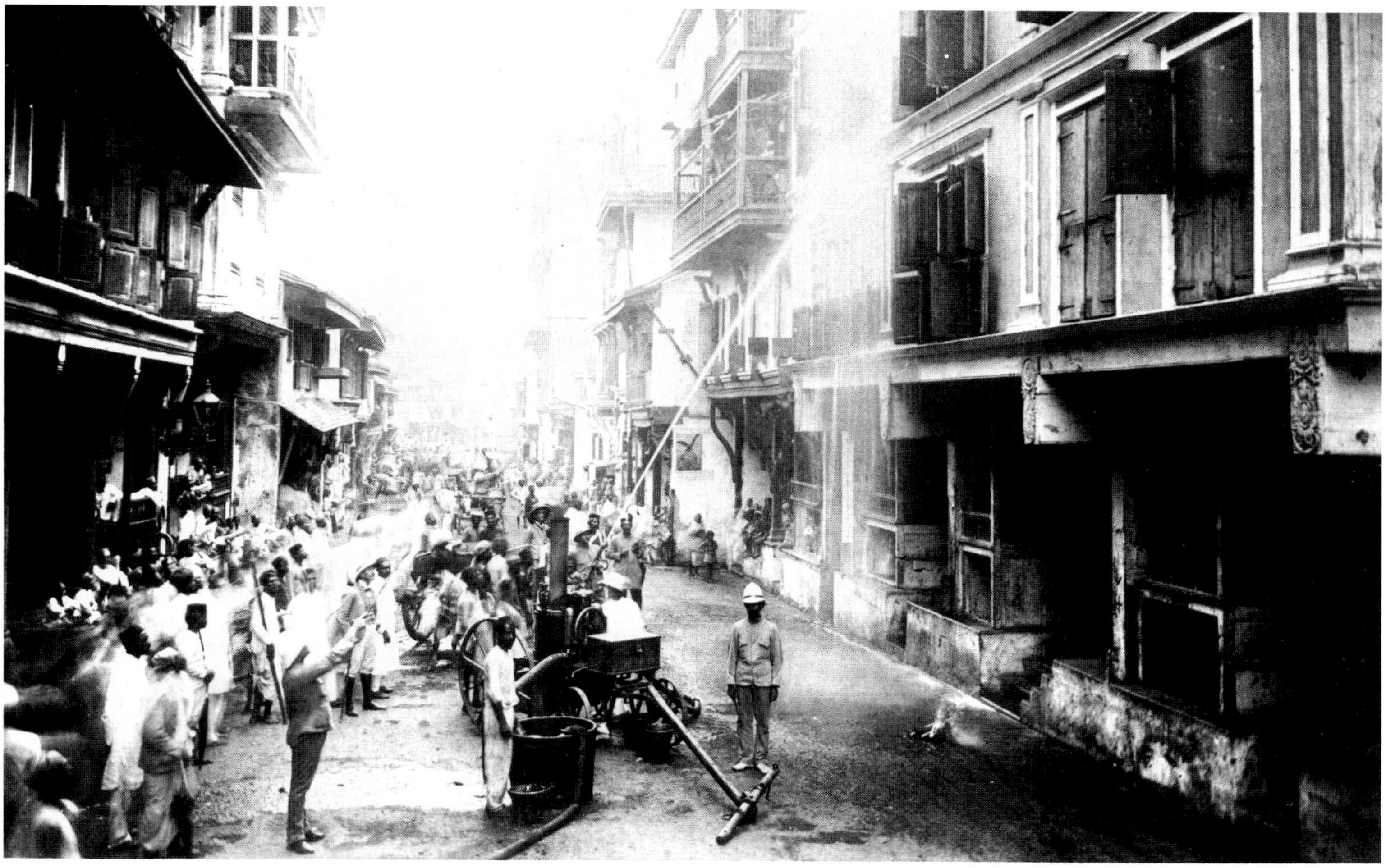

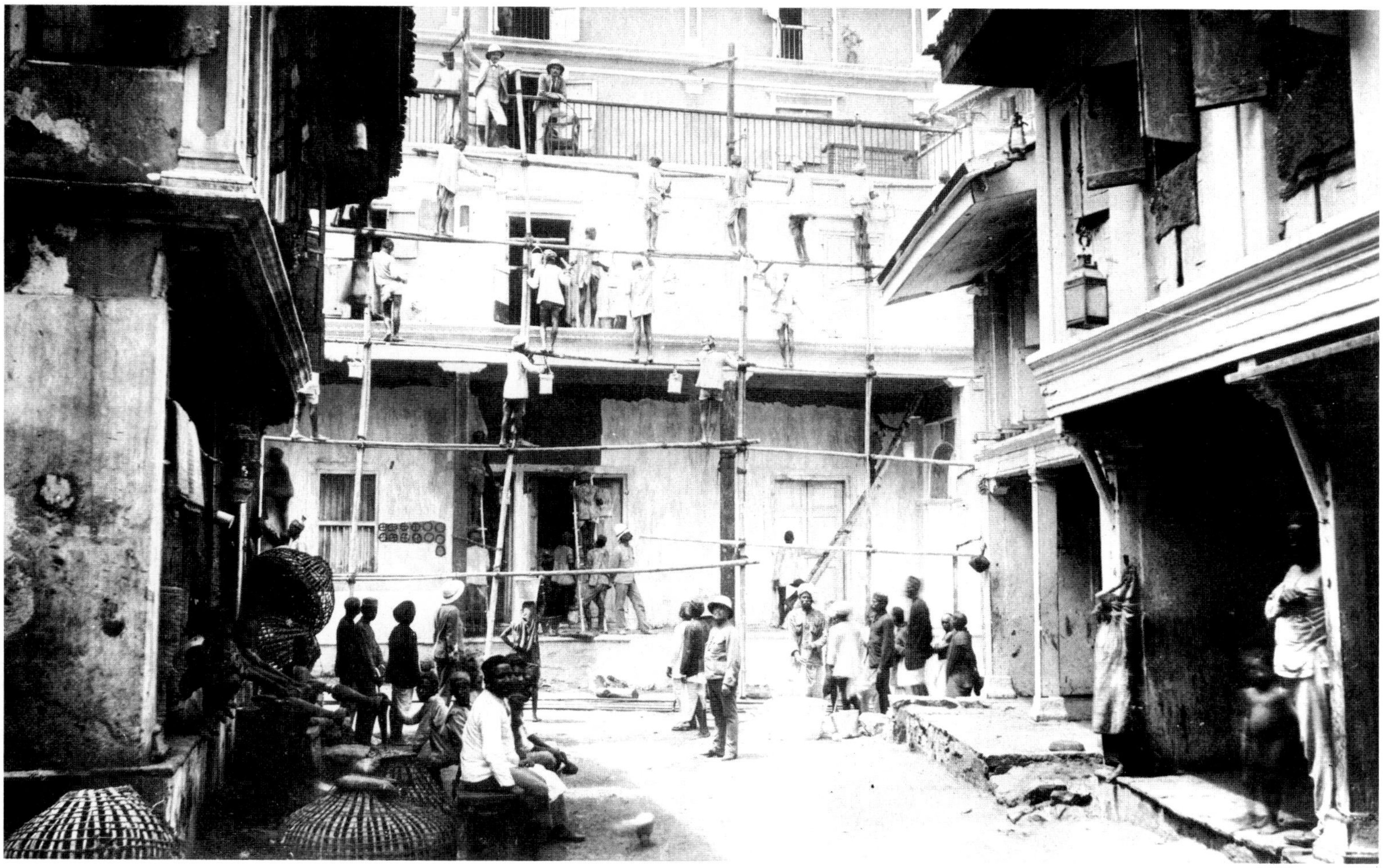

and that it was the government's duty to provide it. The first two government-backed institutions were named after him. Elphinstone High School was founded in 1820 and Elphinstone College in 1828. Both were exclusively for boys (girls' education did not start on a significant scale until the end of the 19th Century) and were endowed with generous grants from Sir Cowasjee Jehangir, one of the city's leading Parsi industrialists. Both institutions are still running under the control of the Bombay government.

They were followed over the next few decades by numerous other schools, both private and public, teaching in both English and Indian languages. The government-backed schools attracted mostly poorer youths from families that had traditionally sought literate occupations, including less wealthy Parsis, certain high-caste Maharashtrian Hindus and some Muslims. The Jesuits opened the St. Xavier School and St. Xavier College to educate Catholics—among them, the children of Indians who had come to Bombay from Portuguese settlements such as Goa, Bassein and Salsette. Bombay University was founded, along with universities in Calcutta and Madras, by the government in 1857; and in the same year the Bombay Art School was opened. Financed by another Parsi, Sir Jamsetjee Jeejeebhoy, it was the first art school in India; and it had J. Lockwood Kipling as its first principal.

That was the year of the Indian Mutiny, when discontent among the *sepoys*—the native soldiers who made up four-fifths of the Indian Army—provoked them to rise against the British in northern India; massacres in Cawnpore and elsewhere led to ferocious retaliation by avenging British troops. The Mutiny hardly affected Bombay. But in its aftermath the extraordinary anachronism was ended whereby a trading concern, the East India Company, was responsible, with some Crown supervision, for ruling vast areas of a great subcontinent. In 1858 the Company's rule was formally brought to an end and the government of India passed exclusively to the British Crown.

In the early decades of Crown rule, Bombay grew dramatically in every way: population, physical extent, employment, wealth, sophistication. By 1896 it had more than 800,000 inhabitants and, despite a serious outbreak of bubonic plague in that year—114,000 people were to die and 43,000 to flee the city—the population soon resumed its growth, passing 900,000 in 1911. Most of this increase had come from immigration, as peasants poured in from rural areas to labour in the booming cotton mills and at the docks. The census of 1901 revealed that more than three-quarters of Bombay's citizens had been born outside the city. It was also a more cosmopolitan city than ever. Thanks to improved transportation, people had arrived from all over India and beyond.

To accommodate the influx, great efforts were made to reclaim parts of Bombay Island that were still swamp. A causeway had already been built

Victoria Terminus, whose vast bulk dwarfs hurrying commuters, was completed in 1888, in a style that subtly combines Gothic and Indian influences.

in 1838 to link the Fort area with Old Woman's Island and Colaba Island, and now attention was turned to the mud-flats north of the Fort. On this land, reclaimed with the help of Indian industrialists who contributed large sums to the enterprise, arose the cotton mills and mill workers' tenements. Meanwhile, in the centre of the Fort area, the great public buildings were plumped down, indicating a new sense of civic pride on the part of both the British and the Indians, who also helped finance these huge monuments.

The machinery of government expanded rapidly, providing plenty of jobs for the graduates of the schools and colleges and university. By the end of the century, Bombay had the highest number of adult male literates in western India and an exceptionally high proportion of them knew English. Most found low-paid clerical jobs in government departments, education and also in industry. But the ambitious among them also found their education a key to social and economic improvement. They often had to struggle to acquire learning, leaving homes on the mainland and suffering hardship and deprivation while they studied. Afterwards they made their mark in government administration and in the professions: law, journalism, medicine and teaching. From their ranks came pioneers of social reform.

Bombay was not only a great imperial city but also the natural headquarters of the Indian nationalist movement. Nationalism grew out of the idealism of the young Indian graduates, and from the need of the rich and influential natives in the city to make their voices heard on political matters. These people became intensely concerned about the formulation of British imperial policy. Where else were people so immediately affected by British decisions about tariffs? Who else matched Bombay's interest in the daily fluctuations in the value of the rupee? Nowhere else in India was there such a concentration of tax-payers, nor so many lawyers and journalists skilled at gathering support for political ends.

On December 28, 1885, a gathering of 72 delegates—mainly Indian lawyers, journalists and schoolmasters, but also some British liberals—met in Bombay and founded the Indian National Congress, India's first national political movement. For the next 30 years the Congress was organized mainly from Bombay. It was financed largely by Bombay merchants and its affairs were dominated by Bombay and Maharashtrian politicians like Pherozeshah Mehta, Gopal Krishna Gokhale and Bal Gangadhar Tilak. In the 1920s and 1930s, too, the Indian National Congress maintained its close connections with Bombay. The politics of cotton, banking and nationalism began subtly but surely to undermine the position of the British in the city and in India as a whole.

It is a paradox that in Bombay—the most Victorian, most British of Indian cities—the British had never been numerically strong and had never succeeded in dominating civic affairs. At the height of empire they displayed a narrow interest in the social round of the governor and his

At the Bombay Yacht Club near Apollo Bunder, a steward sits on the tiled floor to polish the splendid collection of silver trophies that date from the days of the Raj. Founded in 1880 as a preserve of colonial privilege, the Yacht Club did not admit Indians until after Independence. Today the club is one of the few that still provide accommodation for members: the polished wooden name-board on the left lists the occupants and their rooms.

coterie, and practised an aloofness that was both arrogant and obvious. The British had always had their own clubs in India, symbols of their solitude thousands of miles from home. The first of these institutions with its own premises in Bombay was the Byculla Club, founded in 1833; after it came the Bombay Gymkhana in 1875 and the Royal Yacht Club, on the harbour front near Apollo Bunder, in 1880.

These clubs did not admit anyone who was not European. In 1907, there was very nearly a political incident at the Byculla when the Amir of Afghanistan, who had been invited in by a member, was refused service. Then there were the Breach Candy Swimming Baths on the coast at Cumballa. This club originally admitted only white members of the British Empire. Although in the 1930s it eventually widened its terms of reference to include other Europeans, astonishingly it remained closed to Indians. Only a few years ago an Englishwoman married to an Indian businessman took her two children there to swim. She was new, unfortunately, to the paradoxes of Bombay. She was unmistakably white, but her children bore traces of their paternal ancestry. The officials at the pool told her that she could swim but her children could not.

Social exclusiveness in Bombay was not confined to Europeans. All the city's sporting clubs, known as gymkhanas, were run for separate communities. *Khana* in Hindi means "house" and it has been suggested that the word gymkhana came from *gend-khana*—that is, "ball-house" or "racket-court". Later it became confused with the English "gym", short for gymnasium. Both the word and the institution it describes originated in Bombay. Besides the exclusive, Europeans-only Bombay Gymkhana, there were also—and still are—a Hindu, a Muslim, a Catholic and a Parsi gymkhana, flanking one another along Marine Drive as it nears Chowpatty.

Despite these communal and racial divisions, relations between the British and the Indians were always far closer in Bombay than in other Indian cities. The presence of the Westernized Parsis helped to break down the barriers, as did the fact that Indian merchants had contributed so generously to the development of the city. In 1916, when Lord Willingdon was Governor of Bombay, a proposal was made that a new club should be formed open to both British and Indian members. When it was suggested that the club be named after the Governor, Willingdon pointed out with dry humour that in this case the club's initials would be W.C. The dilemma was resolved by the decision to make it the Willingdon Sports Club and to provide sports facilities, including a golf course. J. R. D. Tata, scion of the Parsi family that built the Taj Mahal Hotel, was still toiling around this course every weekend when I was last in Bombay. I can recall him in my childhood, as he set out, accompanied by his caddie, for the links: a small neat man with a kestrel face and pale eyes. My parents and I would be by the swimming pool as he passed, at a table at which both the British and Indians of all castes and creeds sat, sipping pink gins and beers, awaiting the sort of lunch still available now: perhaps fried pomfret with tartare sauce and fresh oysters, followed by "Willingdon Fowl" stuffed with minced pork, chopped liver, eggs and bread.

The Willingdon had not changed much between its foundation and my first experience of it in the 1940s. Nor in some ways had Bombay, despite the rise of nationalist sentiment. At that time Mohammed Ali Jinnah, the leader of the Muslim League and later the founder of Pakistan, a taut, tall, exceptionally well-dressed lawyer, lived on Malabar Hill. My father knew him well. He also knew Gandhi and Jawaharlal Nehru, first Prime Minister of independent India. Both frequently came to Bombay to make speeches when they were not in prison.

In 1942, Gandhi held mass meetings and marches in the city as part of his demand for Britain to "quit India", and riots between the police and nationalists broke out on several occasions. But throughout these heady events the city nevertheless managed to maintain some sense of discipline. During one demonstration, my parents were on their way home from a lunch appointment in the family car, which was, I think, a Wolseley. At this time there were protests by nationalists against the use of imported goods. In a crowded area of the city the car was surrounded by demonstrators. After they had berated my father on the evils of driving in a British car, they told my parents and the chauffeur to climb out of it, since they intended to burn it. My father's arguments carried little weight until he said: "All right. But I don't want my wife to walk home in this heat. Let the chauffeur

Two cricket matches proceed simultaneously on the grassy expanse of the Azad Maidan, an open space in the centre of Bombay. Beyond, rises the massive Municipal Building, housing the offices of the Municipal Corporation. The domed tower is typical of the oriental style adopted by certain late-19th-Century British architects.

drive her home and then come back with the car. I'll wait here with you till it comes back, and then you can burn it."

The rioters were somewhat taken aback by this offer. "We are gentlemen," the leader eventually said. "We won't burn your car. Take your wife home." He offered my father an escort to see the car safely home through the unruly crowds. The escort proved to be excellent protection and, when the car reached home, my father asked them in for a drink. They accepted, drank a lot of imported beer without any apparent disgust and were driven back to where they had come from. The Wolseley returned safely again. Such oddities of behaviour, which were not isolated, seem in retrospect British, not Indian—the relics of standards left over from a lengthy past of inherited conduct.

In 1945 my father was posted abroad and we left Bombay. When we returned in 1948, British rule had ended. The atmosphere of the city had changed, and was to change more: the statues in the streets would be pulled down, the British street-names changed. Recently, when I revisited the library of the Royal Asiatic Society, I found not only that the books were in worse shape than ever, but that the marble busts of British rulers lining the staircase had disappeared. Piles of books were lying around the stately mausoleum in tremendous rotting stacks. The British really had left. Yet, strangely, I found a few British survivors still living in the city more than 30 years after the end of the Raj. One was Roy Hawkins.

After Indian Independence in 1947, he had chosen to stay on in his old job with the Oxford University Press. In his large and beautiful bungalow at the toe of Peddar Road, attended by his faithful Muslim bearer, he provided cigars and whisky for those friends who visited him; and if they wanted to play chess, Hawk was ready. His blue eyes remained as vigilant as ever in a face tanned by frequent walks in the Ghats above Bombay.

In the 1960s Hawk retired and, since he had the remnants of a family in the West of England—they lived in Bath—he had returned to join them. But he was soon homesick and eventually he returned to Bombay, where his old servant awaited him at the airport. (Some years previously, the servant would have awaited Hawk at the docks and collected huge tin trunks rather than Samsonite suitcases.) Hawk then found that his old house had been razed and a huge apartment block built on the site. In this high-rise complex, on the 17th floor, I found him living, peering down upon the city where he had spent most of his life.

From this eminence, staring over brightly lit skyscrapers, he said to me, as his Muslim bearer poured me a drink on his balcony: "Bombay is still the most beautiful place in the world, don't you think?" Though I didn't entirely agree, I respected the opinion of one of the last Englishmen of the old school who wanted to stay in Bombay—a city that the British, through three centuries of effort, had helped to build, defend and provide with a heartbeat of its own.

A Clogged Concourse for Travellers

Heraldic carvings of an elephant and an early steam engine—part of a series decorating V.T.'s exterior walls—illustrate the evolution of Indian transport.

Victoria Terminus, Bombay's biggest railway station (*see pages 54-5*), encompasses within its ornate walls a world with two distinct rhythms. The massive station, locally known as V.T., daily handles nearly 900 trains carrying some two million passengers. On one side of the building, electric trains ferry a hectic army of rush-hour commuters in and out of the city; but on the other side the pace is more leisurely, as long-distance trains, pulled by heavy diesel or steam locomotives, set out across the subcontinent. Fares are among the least expensive in the world, and trains are invariably crowded, so passengers arrive long before departure time to claim their reservations or secure unreserved places. Often carrying baggage and bedding for the journey, they come well prepared to practise the patient art of waiting, a traditional requirement for travel in India.

A long-distance traveller with a reservation in a "ladies only" carriage waits in comfort for departure time. Some trains are fully booked weeks in advance.

Overflowing commuters cling to a crowded electric train arriving at V.T. At rush hour the coaches are often crammed to almost twice their official capacity.

Among groups of passengers who are making themselves comfortable on the stone floor of the station's main concourse, a young man (foreground) leans on his rolled-up mattress. Bedding rolls can be rented at the terminus for use on long, transcontinental journeys.

Behind a group of patient long-distance passengers, others whose reservations are listed on a notice in the window unhurriedly board a departing express.

Whiling away a midday lull, some of V.T.'s 450-strong force of red-uniformed porters snatch a siesta, read newspapers or play cards. The majority of long-distanc

ains leave the terminus between 6 p.m. and midnight, so that—at least for the first part of their journey—passengers can escape the heat and dust of the day.

3

A Diverse Multitude

Bombay contains an astonishing variety of temples, mosques and churches —signposts to the many different ethnic and religious communities in the city. Some of the most notable of these places of worship are prominently sited along the western coast of the island-city. Near the tip of Malabar Point, close to the luxurious apartment blocks of Malabar Hill, stands the Walkeshwar temple complex, a group of Hindu temple buildings and houses for priests that date back to the 11th Century A.D. Walkeshwar ("sand lord") refers to a *lingam*, or phallic symbol of the god Shiva, that was supposed to have been modelled here from sand by the legendary hero Rama; Rama's life is the subject of the *Ramayana*, the great Hindu epic composed long before angels appeared above Bethlehem. Nearby is another sacred spot where Rama, needing to drink, shot an arrow into the earth; water spurted from the cleft earth, enabling him to satisfy his thirst. The spot where the spring is said to have bubbled up is marked by a rectangular, stone-lined water tank called the Banganga. Daily the faithful descend the steps leading to it to purify themselves in the murky water.

Three miles further north, not far from the racecourse, the Hindu temple of Mahalakshmi stands near the Arabian Sea. It is dedicated to Lakshmi, the goddess of wealth; the place, not unnaturally, is particularly sacred to Hindu businessmen. Along a sea-front path nearby, hawkers sell coconuts, flowers and sweets to be offered up by the pious. Inside the temple the carved stone image of the goddess, riding a demon and a tiger in tandem, is draped with jewels, gold bangles and pearl necklaces presented by devotees whose prayers have been satisfied.

North of Mahalakshmi a whitewashed mosque squats in the scurfy sea. It commemorates Haji Ali, a Muslim saint whose tomb is within. At high tide the mosque is islanded amidst waves; but when the sea pulls itself back at low tide, a narrow cement causeway between mainland and mosque is revealed, and is trodden by many worshippers.

A couple of miles beyond, at Worli, the Buddhists have a temple; and on the far headland of the next bay the twin spires of the Basilica of Mount Mary point to the Catholic heaven in the sky. The Basilica is one of a score of Catholic churches in Bombay.

Overlooking Back Bay stands the main temple of the Jains, near Dhobi Ghats—a mossy sprawl of rocks on which *dhobis* (washermen) pound laundry to rinse it, usually to its detriment, before they spread it out for the sun to dry. The Jain sect, founded in the 6th Century B.C., is an offshoot of Hinduism. Like Buddhists, Jains believe in non-violence and have a

In a sacred stone-lined pool, part of the ancient Walkeshwar temple complex on Malabar Hill, a group of Gujarati women—fully dressed to meet the requirements for modesty demanded by Hindu tradition—perform the purification ritual that the devout observe daily. Hindus constitute the largest of the half dozen or so major religious sects in Bombay; they represent almost 70 per cent of the city's population.

A workman reaches down to clean a huge equestrian statue of Shivaji, the 17th-Century founder of the independent Hindu kingdom of Maharashtra. In the 1960s, after Bombay had become the capital of a new Maharashtra State, Shivaji was adopted as the symbol of a local nationalist group, the Shiv Sena or "Army of Shivaji". The movement aimed, unsuccessfully, at driving all non-Maharashtrians from the city.

reverence for all forms of life. The monks wear muslin cloths over their noses and mouths so as not to breathe in the tiniest insect and kill it.

A number of other important shrines are concentrated in central Bombay. Immediately to the west of Horniman Circle stands the Anglican Cathedral of St. Thomas, still the seat of a bishop. Its tall towers have a lonely look—few people apart from foreign tourists frequent it nowadays. In the cobweb of crowded lanes beyond Crawford Market is the largest of the Parsi fire temples in whose inner sancta burn the sacred flames that are worshipped by Parsis as the symbol of God. Elsewhere in the city there are temples, called *gurdwaras*, for the small but growing number of Sikhs from the Punjab, and even a few Jewish synagogues.

Most Bombayites, like most of India's population, are Hindus—nearly 70 per cent of the city's total. Muslims account for about another 15 per cent. That leaves the Christians (mainly Catholics), Buddhists, Jains, Parsis, Sikhs and Jews as tiny, if sometimes very influential, minorities. Despite its numerical superiority, the Hindu majority is fragmented into different communities and has not, therefore, made Bombay what one could call a Hindu city. Hindus have come to Bombay from all over the subcontinent, with different languages and customs as part of their luggage. The Hindus from Maharashtra State itself are the biggest single group (about 45 per cent of the population). Many other Bombayites are distinguished as much by language and origin as by religion. Among them are handfuls of the aboriginal Kolis and Bhandaris; Christians from the former Portuguese colonies of Goa, Salsette and Bassein; as well as a scattering of foreigners, including Arabs, Chinese, Armenians and Europeans.

Given this diversity, communication is something of a problem. Among the Hindus alone the languages spoken include Hindi (the main national language of India, along with English), Marathi, Gujarati, Tamil, Telugu, Sindhi and Kannada. The Muslims speak Gujarati and Urdu (a mixture of Persian and Hindi). The Parsis, having first landed on the Indian sub-continent in Gujarat, speak Gujarati, though with some modifications of their own. The Goan language is Konkani, which is akin to Marathi, with a sprinkling of Portuguese. The local Jews—who are mostly Bene Israel, or "Children of Israel" claiming descent from a handful of Jewish travellers shipwrecked near Bombay in the 2nd Century B.C. —speak Marathi.

For this mixture of millions there has to be a lingua franca. In the Fort area of the city, English is spoken, more or less; it is one of the two official languages of Maharashtra State, the other being Marathi (street signs are written in both). But the further north into the suburbs one goes, the less certain one is of being understood in English. I have often thought that the inhabitants of Bombay are like Cockneys in their sparrow-like resourcefulness and resilience; and over the years they have worked out a means of communication of their own that transcends the city's formidable language barriers. It is a kind of bastard Hindi, sprinkled with Marathi, Gujarati and, most of all, English words; though it horrifies every linguistic purist in India, nearly everyone in Bombay speaks it.

The Westernized, English-speaking upper classes who occupy the high-rise apartments of Colaba, Malabar Hill, Cumballa Hill and Worli Sea Face are not concerned with community divisions. They are far more interested in buying a view, however restricted, of the sea than they are with staying in the same area as their co-religionists, or people from their own state. But for the bulk of the working population, where you live is still largely determined by what language you speak or what religion you practise. Maharashtrians (that is, the original Marathi-speaking inhabitants of Bombay's hinterland who have given their name to the modern state of Maharashtra) tend to be concentrated in the factory areas of Girgaum, Mahim, Dadar, Parel and Andheri; Gujarati Hindus and Jains, in the commercial area of Bhuleshwar; Muslims, in the bazaars of Nagpada, near Crawford Market, in Mahim, and around their mosques; Christians, in Byculla and Bandra; and Parsis in Matunga.

The more recent migrants to the city, from whatever part of the sub-continent they may have come, tend to be the most isolated. Often living in colonies far from the offices and factories where they work, they commute home at the end of the day to the cultural seclusion of their own minority group, surrounded by neighbours and shopkeepers who speak only the language of their place of origin.

Living in a big, overcrowded industrial city creates all kinds of problems for people who have migrated from country areas. For Hindus, lifestyle is very important. Their religion, which has developed and diversified over more than 4,000 years, is not remarkable for its clarity of doctrine. Basic belief in a supreme God is compatible with the worship of one or more of a whole host of *devas* or subsidiary deities. And though traditional Hindu scriptures refer to a divine trinity—Brahma the creator, Vishnu the preserver, and Shiva the destroyer—the most important deities of contemporary worship are rather different. Shiva combines the attributes of creator and destroyer; his consort Parvati is worshipped as Durga, goddess of battle, and Kali, goddess of death. Lakshmi (who is the consort of Vishnu) and Krishna (a human incarnation of Vishnu) are two other important deities.

Hinduism has been described as a way of life rather than of worship. Family life is supposed to be close-knit and the caste system to be respected. Under the extended family system that is part of their tradition, a married couple are expected to share their home not only with their children but with the husband's parents and possibly other relations as well. This traditional arrangement is scarcely possible, however, for poorer families whose only accommodation is in tiny tenement flats.

Caste Hindus are required to take frequent ritual baths; but because many houses have no plumbing, and a solitary tap outside the building, installed by a beneficent government, may serve an entire street, this custom cannot be observed by vast numbers of Bombayites. The lengthy instructions on religion and life that young Hindus are supposed to receive daily— preferably at dusk, in the shade of trees or in spacious rooms as in village tradition—are not easily delivered either. Huddled in hovels, with the electricity constantly fluctuating and the noise of the neighbours providing a continual din, the elders may want to sermonize; but the young don't want to listen. They prefer to plunge into the streets and drift among the crowds. Meanwhile, at home, in front of a cheap picture or a statue of a Hindu deity, a stick of incense smoulders down to ash in a bowl of warm, scented oil; the elders, who still believe or want to, place an occasional flower before the image.

In middle-class households, young Hindus lead an extraordinary double life. Ché Guevara may be the one they worship at school; but Ganesh, the jovial elephant-headed deity so popular in Maharashtra State, is the one they worship at home. There they assume the postures required by their elders. A boy's T-shirt and his deliberately frayed jeans are replaced at home by a loose white shirt, or *kurta*, and baggy white trousers. The girl's mask of lipstick and mascara is whipped off like the mask of a maenad; her low-cut *choli* (tight, short-sleeved blouse) and her "hipster" sari (slung low enough around her hips to reveal rather more than her navel) are replaced by chaste, white cotton clothes.

The tenets of the caste system are by and large adhered to by the bulk of Hindus. The hierarchical structure of Indian society is largely based on this system and is still accepted by many who have been converted, or whose ancestors have been converted, to other religions. The four original Hindu castes were ranked in terms of ritual purity and occupation, with the

Close to Babulnath Temple—a Hindu shrine dedicated to Shiva, the god of destruction and renewal—a woman gains religious merit by feeding a sacred cow. Traditionally revered by Hindus, all cows are protected from slaughter by government edict. The man is weaving garlands of flowers for sale to temple visitors.

Brahmins (priests) at the top, followed by the Kshatriyas (warriors and rulers), the Vaishyas (traders and merchants) and the Sudras (artisans and cultivators). Over the course of the centuries, other subsidiary castes have grown up alongside them to distinguish additional categories of occupation and of rank.

Caste regulates marriage arrangements and even dictates with whom, where and what one may eat. A Brahmin, for example, may not take water from, or food cooked or served by, a member of a lower caste (which explains why so many Brahmins become chefs). Traditionally, members of the lowest Hindu category were outside the caste system; they were regarded as "untouchable" and were ostracized by the rest of society. Today, discrimination against outcastes is illegal in India and those who were once untouchables are now known as "Harijans" or "Children of God", a name coined by Mahatma Gandhi. Rural communities have been slow to accept this innovation and there are villages where Harijans are still forced to live apart from other groups. But in Bombay, where everyone is crowded together in streets and tenements, the traditional distinctions are impossible to preserve with any rigour and Harijans are often indistinguishable from other Hindus.

Indeed, Hindus in Bombay can probably claim greater liberation than elsewhere in India from the sterner Hindu codes of behaviour. Comparatively few wives in the city, for example, wear the *sindhur*, the red powder rubbed into the parting of the hair to indicate that they are married. And although most women still apply the *tika* or *kum-kum*, the small red spot on the forehead (originally, also, a sign of marriage, but now worn purely for decoration), some of the more fashionable change its colour to match that of the sari they are wearing.

Religious customs apart, definite differences of occupation and wealth separate the city's communities. The different Hindu groups are noticeably marked off from one another in this way. Rich Gujarati Hindus, for example, dominate the Stock Exchange and also the Zaveri Bazaar—the gold and diamond market. Maharashtrian Hindus, on the other hand, form the backbone of the city's industrial labour force. Similarly, people of other faiths tend to predominate in certain trades and professions, and to fall into the same income brackets.

By and large, Bombay Muslims today are a lower- and middle-income group. Many of those at the bottom levels work as mill-hands or tailors; some are employed in the slaughterhouses, since no Hindu of caste will spill the blood of animals. These Muslims butcher livestock in the style demanded by Islam: they cut the throat of the living beast and let the blood drain out. The result is *halal* meat (which is similar to kosher meat); and once the oil-prosperous Arabs of the Gulf States realized that so much of the meat in Bombay was butchered in accordance with their own religious principles, they began to import vast quantities. As a consequence,

Clues to a Many-Faceted Urban Society

Like every modern metropolis, Bombay and its population of some eight million make up a complex blend of communities that is reflected in a bewildering array of faces. But to the initiated, appearance and dress can often help to identify the place of a citizen—religious, occupational and ethnic—in the city's varied mix.

The good-luck amulet on the wrist of the youth (top row, left) reveals that he is a Hindu who has participated in a traditional ceremony; the white habit of the girl (middle row, centre) is that of a novice nun of Mount Mary Convent; and the elaborate gold jewellery of another girl (middle row, right) has been donned for a festival of the wealthy Jain sect. Less ostentatious jewellery is worn by the woman (bottom row, left) who has applied two *tikas*—decorative red Hindu marks— to her forehead.

There are, of course, the usual insignia of modern urban roles: the red beret worn by the teenage girl (top row, centre) indicates her responsibility as a school road-safety guard; the grubby cap and shirt of the *hatgariwalla*, or porter equipped with his handcart, are typical dress of the Bombay manual worker; while in smart contrast to it is the uniform cap of the police sergeant (middle row, left).

And finally, the carefully folded turban-like *pughri* designates an elderly Parsi priest (bottom row, centre), whose characteristic keen features are shared with a Parsi woman shopkeeper (bottom row, right).

in addition to its many other problems, Bombay in recent years has suffered a shortage of fresh meat, and prices for it have risen steeply.

Apart from this sanguinary vocation, many Muslims are in trade. Off Mohamedali Road, which runs north from Crawford Market, is perhaps the most interesting area where Muslims trade and live. It is called Chor Bazaar, or Thieves' Market, not only because some of the items on sale may have been stolen, but because some of the merchants sell fakes.

At the mouth of one of the district's narrow, muddy alleys—crowded with people on foot, bicycles and scooters—is a shop of surprisingly sophisticated appearance, with glass doors and display cases. Its owners obtain, in one way or another, original handbags by Gucci, Yves St. Laurent, Dior and other internationally famous designers. They then set their own skilled workmen to making copies of these handbags, down to the monogram. Their relatively inexpensive counterfeits sell extremely well, of course, to Bombay's society women. Surrounding shops specialize in leather products whose designs have not been pirated.

Not long ago on a visit to the Chor Bazaar I was particularly struck by another area containing a huddle of shops whose main items of merchandise were used bathtubs and lavatory bowls. There was also a section that sold crockery, most of it slightly chipped, and another that dealt in furniture, some in beautiful carved rosewood. Among the crockery and the furniture were items that looked valuable, but a friend who was accompanying me disabused me of this idea. "These chaps," he said, "are extremely clever. They know what people think is fashionable from one year to the next and they have their own workmen make whatever is especially in demand. The small defects are deliberately added to persuade customers that they are getting a bargain." Occasionally, though, people who visit the bazaar in search of antiques are rewarded: I visited the house of some well-to-do people in Bombay that featured a pair of really fine Victorian crystal chandeliers and my hostess took a certain pride in announcing that they came from Chor Bazaar.

A curious feature of the neighbouring Bhendi Bazaar is the Raudat Tahera Mosque, erected in 1973 as a mausoleum for a former, much-loved spiritual leader of a Muslim sect to which many of the local businessmen belong. Despite the decrepit appearance of their stalls and themselves, the traders are not impecunious and their donations contributed to the creation of a very special kind of edifice: a palatial marble mosque built on the lines of the Taj Mahal in Agra. From the ceiling of its air-conditioned entrance hall hang innumerable crystal chandeliers flown in, so I am told, from Italy. The doors are of silver and the walls are inscribed in pearls, diamonds and gold with quotations from the Koran.

A little way from Chor Bazaar is a street inhabited by Muslims who make and sell perfumes. From time immemorial, well-to-do Indians—men as well as women—have tended to smother themselves in scent, usually of a

On Chowpatty Beach, a Hindu priest conducts a short, annual ceremony in which men and boys of the Brahmin caste replace the sacred cotton thread each always wears around his body. The first threads, made of several strands of spun cotton, are given to them between the ages of six and 11, as a symbol of their initiation into Hinduism's highest caste. The bands on some celebrants' wrists mark another Hindu festival.

very musky kind. While an exceptionally rich Bombayite may anoint herself or even himself lavishly with, say, Chanel No. 19, those who are financially less well endowed use the scents concocted in the market district. In front of the row of scent shops that shoulder one another down this noisy street, there are racks of bottles on display ranging in size from the kind of small phial that the Borgias probably emptied into the wine of an unwary enemy to bottles the size of vacuum flasks.

On wooden platforms behind the racks of bottles sit the proprietors. As soon as a customer appears, the proprietor wraps a small piece of cotton-wool round the end of a toothpick, dips it into a vessel and hands it to the customer to sniff. The scents range widely in colour and are oddly named: "Sweet Heart", "Macro", and "Saucy Boque" (I take the latter to mean Bouquet), to offer a few examples. A box lined in imitation velvet and containing six small bottles of different scents costs perhaps Rs 30 (or about $3.75). Once a purchase has been made, the customer is presented with a plastic rose saturated in perfume.

Bombay has a particularly wide variety of Muslim sects. As the first major port of call for ships arriving from the Middle East, it received large numbers of Muslim traders and missionaries. The dominant group, as elsewhere on the subcontinent, are the Sunnis (the branch to which the Mughal emperors belonged); they are the orthodox adherents of the caliphate set up to succeed the prophet Muhammad when he died in A.D. 632. The Shi'ah, a breakaway sect whose members challenge the line of succession, are also present in substantial numbers and are further divided into Bohras, Khojas and other minor subdivisions. There are two groups of Khojas and the major branch follow the Aga Khan. In 1936, on the fiftieth anniversary of his accession to the title, the late Aga Khan III visited Bombay, where he was weighed upon a pair of oversized scales and balanced by a heap of gold. The gold represented tribute donated by his followers around the world and, since he did not stint himself in the matter of food, the amount of gold required to balance the scales was, to say the least, considerable. Afterwards, the money was put into trust for the benefit of the faithful. The Aga Khani Khojas have never been noticeably troubled by poverty.

The Catholic community, on the other hand, possibly has the highest ratio of chronic unemployment in the city. It is divided into two groups that are by no means brotherly towards each other: the East Indians, originally inhabitants of the Portuguese colonies at Bassein and Salsette, and the Goans. The Goans originally came to Bombay in substantial numbers after the Second World War to look for work; there was never much to be obtained under the Portuguese, who made little effort to develop the Goan economy. They tend to be of darker complexion than the East Indians, have a reputation for enjoying drink (their favourite beverage being *feni*, a liquor made from cashew fruit or coconuts) and tend towards service occupations—working intermittently, for example, as cooks, butlers and ship's stewards. The East Indians, unlike the Goans, are often fair of skin and, as a result of characteristic diligence, are likely to be property-owning and well-to-do.

Members of the city's Catholic community are among those who still honour the old Hindu caste system, despite the fact that centuries may have passed since their forebears were converted by the Portuguese. The East Indians usually claim to be descended from Brahmins—and Brahmins only. When my father, whose ancestors came from Goa, wanted to marry my mother, an East Indian, both Catholic families were initially opposed to the wedding. One reason, on the part of my maternal grandparents, was that my father was not only a Goan but a Kshatriya, whereas my mother was supposed to be Brahmin and therefore of higher caste.

Most of the Catholics in central Bombay live in cramped slum flats, from whose narrow windows flags of drying laundry flutter. They are clustered either in Colaba around Wodehouse Cathedral, an elegant 20th-Century edifice in grey stone, or in Byculla and Mazagaon, cluttered districts on the other side of the Fort area.

They also inhabit one or two little-known enclaves. A friend once showed me, in the back lanes of the congested district of Girgaum, a tiny Catholic colony of houses built in the Portuguese style, with latticed-iron windows and sturdy tiled roofs. The place was closed off by narrow lanes from the clamour of the road beyond and had an aura of utter silence and peace. In Mazagaon I have seen a similar colony, a centre of quiet amidst streets crammed with blaring cars. These two Catholic colonies may be the last of their kind left in the inner city and will perhaps not survive long.

Catholic middle-class families live mostly in Santa Cruz, near Bombay airport; or in Bandra, the district in which the Basilica of Mount Mary stands. Their small houses are always whitewashed, a habit that may have been formed when the Portuguese decreed that every house in their Indian possessions should be whitewashed once a year.

Although the Catholics of Bombay have, of course, produced men of remarkable achievement, I sense a general feeling of stagnation in the community. The lassitude of those who work at menial jobs is one obvious sign of it. Nevertheless, there are very few destitute Catholics in the city. For the indigent the Church provides accommodation, food, clothes and, occasionally, money. Moreover, most Catholics who find themselves in temporary, or even permanent, financial embarrassment can usually count on support from other branches of their family.

The community best known for looking after their own, however, are the Parsis. It is virtually impossible for a Parsi to starve in Bombay. There are Parsi charities, Parsi organizations to distribute food to the poor, and Parsi schools and hospitals admission to which is free or at a nominal fee.

Celebrating the spirited summer festival of Gokul Ashtami, several lively youngsters form a precarious human pyramid. It will enable an agile member of the crowd to capture a pot suspended high above street-level that contains curds mixed with coins. The festival marks the birth of Krishna (an incarnation of the Hindu deity Vishnu, the preserver) whose youthful pranks are narrated in many Indian legends.

In the Bombay home of a Parsi family, four
priests conduct an annual ceremony to honour
deceased relatives. In accordance with the
Zoroastrian faith that the original Parsis
brought from their native Persia, each priest
wears a mask to avoid defiling by his breath
the food prepared for the ritual and, since fire
is sacred, the flames of the censer and candles.

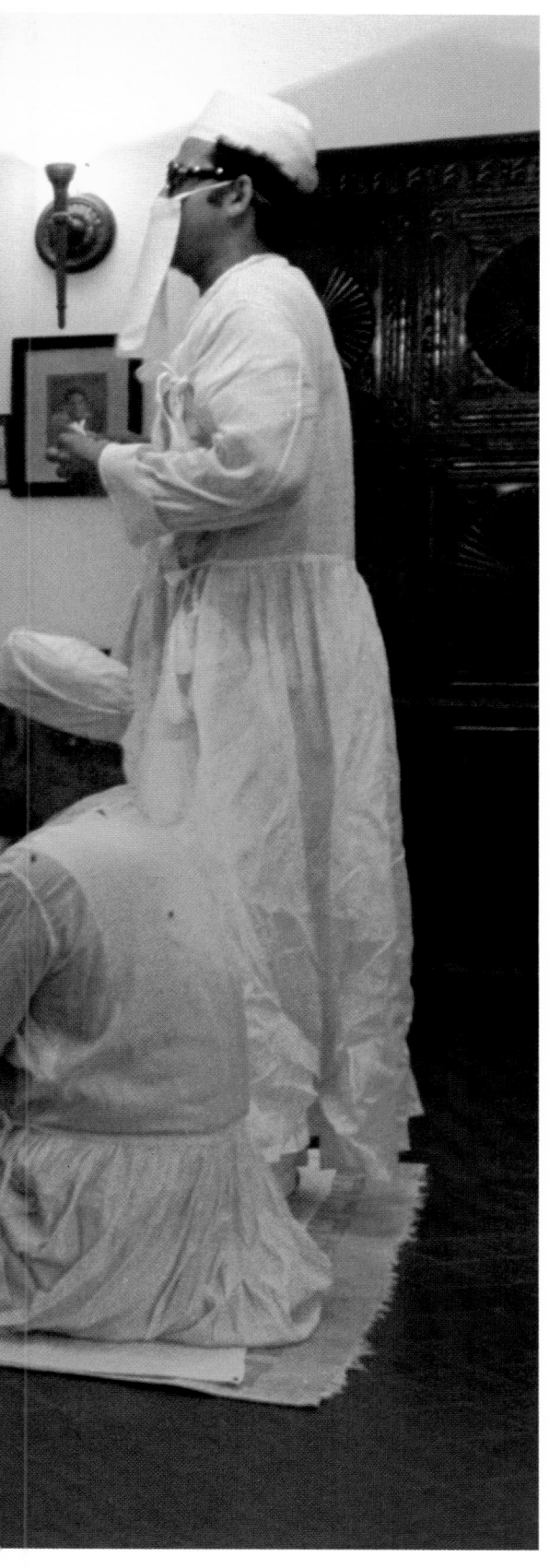

Parsi apartment blocks have been built for the old and poor who have retired on tiny pensions: there is a large one, austere but adequate, on Colaba Causeway. All these projects have been subsidized by the wealthy Parsi families, some of whom (the Tatas for example) are very rich indeed.

When the original Parsi migrants from Iran landed at Sanjan, on the coast of Gujarat, in the 8th Century, the local Raja is reputed to have told their high priest that he could admit only a few of the refugees into his small fiefdom. Symbolically, therefore, he presented the priest with a bowl full to the brim of milk. The priest thereupon took a small coin and dropped it in the bowl. Brim-full though it was, not a drop of milk over-flowed. The Raja, who seems to have been much addicted to symbolism, accepted this as a sign that there was room for all the Parsis and allowed them to settle. Another version of the story has it that the Parsi high priest dissolved a spoonful of sugar in the milk, to signify the unobtrusive but valuable contribution his community could make to their adopted land.

The Parsis have always been a small, closely knit community. In Bombay, which has the largest Parsi community not only in India but in the world, they number only about 80,000. Since the departure of the British they have been showing signs of decline. Various factors appear to threaten the community's survival. The Parsis have always tended to marry among themselves, with the result that an inordinately high percentage of their children are born with physical or mental defects and their fertility has fallen to a low level. Another reason for the low birth rate is that Parsi men and women who are taking up professional careers often marry late. Furthermore, the older Parsi businessmen—with their genteel, anglicized methods—are retiring into a dignified but *passé* aristocracy, living comfortably off their accumulated wealth. Their commercial empires have been usurped by aggressive Hindus from Sind and by Marwaris from Rajasthan. Most of their huge Victorian mansions have either been demolished to make way for high-rise apartments or bought by Hindus.

Interestingly, a survey in the late 1970s showed that a number of Parsis, notably the young ones, would like to leave the city of their forefathers. They wanted to go, not to other places in India, but abroad, preferably to countries such as Britain, America, Canada and Australia, where Parsi communities are already established.

Even the Parsis' funerary rites—such a key feature of their Zoroastrian religious practice—are beginning to change. The ancient Zoroastrians regarded fire, earth and water as sacred elements, and therefore not to be defiled. So they left their dead on mountain tops, for the attentions of vultures and other scavengers. In Bombay, modern Parsi ritual still requires the exposure of the dead in *dakhmas* ("receptacles for the dead"), the euphemistically known "towers of silence". Located in a small, forested section of Malabar Hill known as Doongarwadi, the towers may be entered only by a handful of hereditary pall-bearers. Each tower is actually a

Citadels of the Vultures

Clustered on the crown of Malabar Hill and hidden from below by dense vegetation are seven circular walled enclosures—the so-called towers of silence (*dakhmas* or "receptacles for the dead"), where Bombay's Parsis leave their cadavers to be devoured by vultures.

The Parsis' traditional method of corpse disposal probably pre-dates the origin of their religion, some 2,500 years ago, but it was reinforced when the prophet Zoroaster enjoined his followers not to defile the three sacred elements: earth, fire and water. The dead could, therefore, be neither buried nor cremated.

After a funeral service, held either in the home or in a pavilion near the *dakhma*, hereditary bearers carry the corpse into the enclosure and lay it out naked in a designated place. Once the body has been picked clean by the vultures, the bones are thrown into a central pit lined with sand and charcoal to filter the rain-water and avoid polluting the earth.

Within the high walls of a dakhma, four professional pall-bearers carry a Parsi corpse to its place on the platform, there to await the attentions of the vultures.

massive circular platform of stone about 30 yards in diameter, sloping gently down to a central pit and protected by a high wall. Gardens and palm trees seal them off from prying eyes. Large vultures circle overhead, flapping down whenever a new body has been laid out for them. After the vultures have finished with a corpse, the bones are thrown into the central pit, where they gradually disintegrate.

In recent years the *dakhmas* have been a major source of controversy within the Parsi community. The orthodox maintain that this method of corpse disposal is efficient and sanitary; but some reformers claim that Bombay's vulture population is declining and that corpses are therefore sometimes simply left to putrefy. Residents of the new, high-rise apartment blocks nearby also complain that occasional undesirable pieces are dropped on their balconies by the vultures. The controversy is further complicated by the value of land in this sought-after residential area; many property speculators would dearly love to obtain the sites of the towers and the surrounding gardens for redevelopment. Nowadays some Parsis choose to cremate their dead and the trend may gather pace.

Each Bombay community has its own religious festivals; and since people of all faiths usually get the day off on such occasions, the city perhaps has more public holidays than any other in the world. The members of the different communities tolerate and even enjoy, if only as spectators, the celebrations of other faiths. Some festivals are peculiar to Bombay, but others—such as the Hindu observances of Holi, Gokul Ashtami, Diwali and Dasahra—are common throughout India. Of these, Holi—the spring festival in February or March, derived from an ancient fertility rite—is literally the most colourful. People rush around wearing their oldest clothes and carrying paper bags full of coloured powder, or water-pistols loaded with coloured water, which they throw or squirt at anyone within reach.

Gokul Ashtami, which celebrates the birthday of the god Krishna, takes place in August. Earthenware pots containing a mixture of curds and coins are strung up high across the streets and young men form human pyramids in attempts to reach the pots and overturn them. The coins provide the youths with an incentive and the curds symbolize Krishna's fondness for dairy products. (He is said to have been brought up as a cowherd and to have had a predilection for milkmaids.)

Dasahra, early in October, lasts 10 days and celebrates an episode in the *Ramayana*. It tells how Ravana, the demon king of Sri Lanka (Ceylon), kidnapped Rama's beautiful wife Sita and took her to his kingdom. At this point, Rama and his devoted younger brother Lakshmana befriended Hanuman, lord of the monkeys. Hanging on to one another's tails, Hanuman's acrobatic animals formed a living bridge across the Palk Straits that separate India from Sri Lanka; whereupon the brothers crossed over, killed Ravana and his fellow demons, and rescued Sita. During

In a garlanded silver coach drawn by bullocks, elaborately adorned Jains—members of one of Bombay's smaller sects, an offshoot of Hinduism established in the 6th Century B.C.—ride in procession to one of their temples. The parade takes place at the conclusion of Paryushana, an annual eight-day period of fasting, undertaken as a sign of both self-discipline and atonement.

Dasahra, this story is celebrated by a re-enactment of the trials and the eventual triumph of Rama, culminating in the slaying of Ravana. Gigantic cardboard and papier-mâché figures of all the demons tower over the parks of Bombay until the last night of the festival when, in a blaze of fireworks and flames, the leering figures are consumed by fire.

Diwali, the Festival of Lights some three weeks after Dasahra, honours Lakshmi, goddess of wealth, and is regarded by some Hindus, especially traders, as the onset of the New Year. It is celebrated with fireworks of all sorts; Bombay during Diwali looks and sounds like a city under siege. There are continual whirring and shrieking noises, punctuated by huge detonations and rockets streaking like tracer bullets across the sky. Badly made or carelessly lit fireworks cause accidents every year, but Diwali remains a very popular festival. Taxi-drivers hang garlands on their rickety vehicles, in thanks for having been of service during the old year; factory workers do the same with their machines; and businessmen and shop-keepers open up their account books, making sure as an auspicious start to the New Year that a credit balance is indicated.

Two Hindu festivals are especially popular in Bombay and both are connected with the sea. In August, towards the end of the monsoon season, Nariel Purnima—Coconut Day—comes around. Rain may still fall, but the weather is unlikely to be vehement enough to capsize a boat; it is, therefore, time for fishing to recommence. In oblation to their vessels, the fishermen burn little oil lamps, break coconuts on the bows and throw flowers into the bottom of each boat. They also drift coconuts away at low tide as an offering to the sea. These coconuts serve an additional, practical purpose inasmuch as the tide, as it turns, brings some of them back to the shore for the city's beggars to eat. During Nariel Purnima, Chowpatty and the outlying beaches are densely crowded with onlookers.

Ganesh Chaturthi—the birthday of the elephant-headed god Ganesh, son of Shiva and Parvati—arrives, like Coconut Day, towards the end of the monsoon season, in August or September. Huge effigies of the god, and smaller ones of his parents and attendants, are paraded through the city to the musical accompaniment of conches, drums, trumpets and flutes. Then—at the seashore, after prayers and the burning of incense—the garlanded figures are surrendered, in a symbolic act, to the purifying waves. Ganesh is variously revered as the remover of obstacles (he is worshipped by Hindus at the start of any new undertaking) and the lord of the intellect, of artisans and artists. He is also the god of prosperity. His elephant's head has been explained in many colourful legends, all of which relate to his boyhood. In one version, his own head was cut off in anger by Shiva, who was never known for his placid temperament; in another it was shattered into pieces by other envious deities; while in a third, it was incinerated by an inadvertent glance from Sani (Saturn). After-wards, Shiva promised Parvati to replace the boy's head with that of the

During a festival in central Bombay's Sonapur district, a Catholic matron supervises the procession of little girls who are responsible for strewing petals before an image of Our Lady of Dolores. Catholicism, introduced into India by Portuguese settlers in the 16th Century, is the predominant faith among the 5 per cent of the city's population who are Christians.

**Outside the Catholic Church of Mount Mary in
the northern suburb of Bandra, a candle-seller
makes flower garlands for the devout to offer
the Virgin. The candles, cast in the shape of the
human body or parts of it, are lit in supplication,
an act accompanied by prayers requesting
that the Virgin will cure an affliction in the
corresponding place on the worshipper's body.**

first living thing he came across. It was an elephant. Shiva made his wife
another promise: he would make her son the leader of his *ganas* or
demigods. Ganesh means lord of the *ganas*.

In the early years of this century the Maharashtrian nationalist leader
Bal Gangadhar Tilak exploited Ganesh Chaturthi for his own political
ends. At the time, political meetings were banned by the British. Tilak
revived the popularity of the Ganesh festival and to the masses of people
who gathered to celebrate he preached the message of independence
from the British Raj. Since those times the birthday of Ganesh has
retained its local popularity and in Bombay it is celebrated by almost
everyone, whether Hindu or not.

Other religious festivals tend to be less colourful. The Parsis, for example,
have no religious processions, a tradition that probably dates back to the
terms on which they were first admitted into India by the Raja of Sanjan.
Instead, they eat. Uninhibited feasting is the hallmark of a Parsi festival;
and occasions for such indulgence are frequent, since Parsi banquets are
not confined to religious days but follow all weddings and the Navjote
ceremonies when children are initiated into the Zoroastrian faith. The
Navjote, analogous to a Jewish barmitzvah or batmitzvah, remains an
essential and formidable ceremony for all young Parsis. It takes place when
a child is nine to 10 years old, by which time he or she is supposed to have
memorized most of the Parsi prayer-book. Since the prayers are in
Pahlavi, the ancient language of Persia, they are unintelligible to the
majority of children and have to be learnt parrot-fashion. At this solemn
ceremony, attended by relatives and friends (including non-Parsis), the

Shi'ah Muslims, some of them blood-stained from self-inflicted wounds, chant the name of Imam Husain—the grandson of the prophet Muhammad—during a procession in the Islamic month of Muharram that marks his death. Others (inset) flagellate themselves until their backs are running with blood. The Shi'ah, largest of Islam's minority sects, believe that Husain was the rightful successor to the prophet Muhammad.

nervous novice chants the prayers and is invested by the priests with the *sudrah* (sacred undershirt) and *kusti* (sacred lamb's-wool thread wound around the waist), both of which orthodox Parsis wear at all times. Once the ordeal is over, the food-loving guests descend on huge dishes of rice, fish, meat and custards prepared in the Parsi style. Leftover food is usually distributed to the hundreds of starving people who always collect outside the place where a Parsi banquet is being held.

The main Muslim religious spectacle in Bombay occurs during the Islamic lunar month of Muharram, after which the celebration is named. (Since the Muslim year is shorter than the solar one of 365 days, Muharram is related to no single month in the Western calendar.) In A.D. 680 on the 10th of Muharram, Muhammad's grandson Husain was killed in battle on the banks of the River Euphrates; his brother Hasan had died, allegedly poisoned, 12 years earlier. To mourn the deaths of the two brothers, Bombay Muslims fast for 10 days before taking *taziyas*, or replicas of Husain's tomb (actually located at Karbala in Iraq), in procession through Mohamedali Road and other Muslim areas, eventually immersing the *taziyas* in the sea, which is symbolic of the Euphrates.

Participants in the Muharram procession dance in a frenzy of grief, beating their breasts, flagellating themselves and chanting *"Ya Hasan! Ya Husain!"* (O Hasan! O Husain!) in memory of the two brothers. These words were corrupted by English ears to "Hobson-Jobson" and found their way into the English language—and the English dictionary—as a phrase meaning "native festal excitement". The eminent lexicographers Henry Yule and Arthur Burnell considered "Hobson-Jobson" to be such an appealing example of this kind of verbal modification that they adopted it as a light-hearted alternative title to their *Glossary of Anglo-Indian Colloquial Words and Phrases*, published in 1886 and still a standard work on the subject.

Bombay Catholics have their own important festival: the annual feast of Mount Mary in Bandra, during which processions of worshippers toil up the long, steep road to the church. The sides of the road are lined with stalls selling aerated drinks and food, and women selling wax candles, some of which are made in the shape of the human body or of various parts of it. Sick people, or their relatives, buy candles shaped like the afflicted parts and burn them at the altar, offering up prayers for recovery. The Bandra feast, which continues for some days, does not attract only Catholics; people of all communities come to it, though more for the spectacle it presents than for any spiritual reason.

Bombay's ethnic and religious groups have not always lived peacefully together. There has always been friction in the subcontinent between the two major religious groups, Hindus and Muslims; and in Bombay, shortly before and after Partition in 1947, this animosity led to some violent incidents. In the late 1950s and the 1960s, a hostility of another sort emerged between Maharashtrians and non-Maharashtrians. Bombay's Maharashtrians were not, as a rule, well off. They resented the wealth and power of the city's élites: not just the older-established Parsis and Gujaratis, but the upstart Sindhis and Marwaris as well. A further irritant was a steady immigration into the city of young people from the south where, especially in the state of Kerala, the standard of literacy was considerably higher than in other Indian states. Few white-collar jobs were available in the south, which was not highly industrialized and depended mainly on its fisheries and agriculture; so the young college graduates there came to fulfil Bombay's ever-increasing need, as a commercial metropolis, for secretaries, clerks, office workers, stenographers and the like. Because the southerners were generally better qualified for these posts, they tended to be given preference over young Maharashtrians who, unless they were very lucky, had to accept menial work whatever their level of education. (I recall that a Maharashtrian office boy who for a long time ran errands for my father was a graduate in economics.)

A new blow to the Maharashtrians' shaken sense of identity came in the 1950s. Immediately after Independence, the old Bombay Presidency had been superseded by a new geographical entity, Bombay State, that reached out to encompass both present-day Maharashtra State and present-day Gujarat State, with their two distinctive language groups. When, in 1956, proposals were made to redraw all of India's state boundaries along linguistic lines, Bombay State was excluded from the plan. Taking exception to this exception, the Maharashtrians swarmed into the streets of Bombay and serious riots broke out. Later, when it was announced that Bombay State would be eliminated and that the new political structure would consist of the two original linguistic units after all, further problems emerged: the Gujaratis claimed that, since Bombay was an industrial city and, since a large percentage of its industries were owned by Gujaratis, it should be declared a separate city-state on its own—a proposal that was not adopted. At last, in 1960, Bombay became the capital of the current Maharashtra State.

Logically, perhaps, the term "Maharashtrian" should now cover all Bombayites, but it does not; it retains its specific application to the original Marathi-speaking Hindus. And unfortunately the grievances of this community were not wholly allayed by the creation of the new state; local politicians were too dependent on the non-Maharashtrian business community to pay much attention to the indigenous majority. Then, in 1966, as the effects of an economic recession were being felt, the Maharashtrians found a leader: Bal Thackeray, a short, bespectacled, excitable man. Thackeray had been a rather unsuccessful political cartoonist but discovered in himself a talent for oratory. He capitalized on it. Maharashtra, he said, should be for the Maharashtrians alone—a slogan that if taken

Gathered on the expanse of the Azad Maidan, Muslims wait to participate in the broadcast prayers that will end Ramadan, Islam's annual month of fasting.

In a side-street outside the Raudat Tahera Mosque in Bhendi Bazaar, members of an overflowing Friday congregation bring other activity to a halt as they bow towards Mecca after a prayer. Friday is the Muslim Sabbath.

literally would have meant the eviction from Bombay of the wealthy Gujarati industrialists and other providers of employment for local people.

Thackeray and his followers, who called themselves the Shiv Sena or "Army of Shiva" after Shivaji, the 17th-Century Maratha leader, directed their campaign primarily at the South Indians who, they felt, were depriving them of a livelihood: in their view the South Indians should be sent back to their home states. Soon the Shiv Sena decided on aggressive action against the defenceless South Indian settlements. They looted and sometimes burnt down houses and shops, and the police, themselves predominantly Maharashtrian, did little to stop the violence.

To demonstrate their control of the city, the Shiv Sena from time to time proclaimed a *bandh* (general strike), ordering shops, offices and public services to close down for a day; their threats of violent reprisals against recalcitrants ensured obedience. By such means, and by a tough anti-Communist stance that endeared them to some of the city's industrialists and Congress Party politicians, they had gathered enough support by 1968 to win a significant number of seats in the city's governing body, the Bombay Municipal Corporation. Due to their new influence in civic affairs, educated Maharashtrians in increasing numbers were hired for white-collar office and secretarial posts once largely filled by South Indians.

Although the Shiv Sena was an entirely parochial party and Bombay its only parish, Thackeray attempted to turn it into a national political force. In the 1971 general election for India's federal parliament, the Shiv Sena put up seven candidates in the Bombay constituencies. Because of the mixed composition of these constituencies and stiff competition from national parties with more money and popular appeal, the Shiv Sena failed to win any of the seats. After this failure, although remaining active at the grass-roots level of Bombay's political life, the Shiv Sena lost its momentum, apparently irretrievably.

In the history of Bombay the importance of the Shiv Sena's campaign is that it has been the only serious attempt to change the cosmopolitan nature of the city, and that it failed. Language, custom and religion may divide the people into sects and communities, as they do in the rest of India; but in Bombay such group loyalties are compatible with a wider allegiance. Each citizen recognizes that he belongs not only to his own community but to the city; he is that distinctive breed, the Bombayite.

Effigies for a God of Good Fortune

Nude plaster-of-Paris models, later to be costumed as deities to accompany Ganesh, receive lifelike paint in a back-street workshop open to onlookers.

Bombay's most popular annual festival marks the birthday of Ganesh, the elephant-headed god of luck, intellect and plenty. Hindu legend offers various explanations for his elephant's head. In the most common, his father Shiva beheaded him in a fit of rage and then, to answer the pleas of Ganesh's mother Parvati, gave him the head of the first living creature he could find: an elephant. For weeks before the festival begins, Bombay craftsmen are busy creating clay statuettes of Ganesh, for private sale, and building large plaster-of-Paris figures, commissioned by clubs and associations. Other images are created to represent Parvati and Shiva, as well as associated gods and saints. On the festival's final day more than two million celebrators join the procession as the effigies are carried to the city's beaches and, following Hindu custom, are immersed in the sacred waters.

Artisans add final touches to two images of Ganesh, who traditionally has more than the usual quota of arms.

Workmen adjust the crown of a giant, 30-foot-high effigy of Ganesh, commissioned by a local political party to grace the procession on the festival's last day.

SREE GANESH COLD-DRI

Seated in the cup of a lotus flower, symbol of
divine birth, the giant representation of Ganesh
illustrated on the previous page passes through
the Parel industrial district (left) on its day-long
progress towards the sea. Other statues in the
procession include a glamorous version of the
god's mother Parvati (above), adorned with
costume jewellery and garlands of flowers.

At sunset Chowpatty Beach is packed, as worshippers crowd the tideline and wade into the sea to bid farewell to Ganesh (centre) and his various companions.

At low tide the morning after the festival, an effigy of Sai Baba, a popular saint, and next to it a small figure of Shiva, have come to rest with startling effect.

Damaged but still serene, the disembodied plaster-of-Paris head of one of Ganesh's companions sticks up in the shallows among wading children.

Its garlands blackened by sea water, a small pot-bellied image of Ganesh floats off Chowpatty Beach, opposite the high-rise buildings of central Bombay.

4

Life in the Dark Depths

Only a few years ago, a traveller who arrived for the first time at Bombay's Santa Cruz Airport looked around him—if his curiosity overcame his exhaustion—and could see misty blue hills to the north, and around the airport area flat fields with occasional trees. Humped, underfed cattle were at pasture in the fields and from time to time they would amble across the runway, a hazard to any pilot trying to land or take off, so that they had to be chased away by the ground crews. In the airport lobby there were doe-eyed women in saris, awaiting the arrival of relatives or friends, or their own departure. Large, colourful posters on the lobby walls purported to show what India was really like: full of temples, palaces, forts, snow-helmeted mountains, forests of exotic flora and fauna, white beaches fringed with palm trees and blue waves beyond.

At that point, more likely than not, the tourist suffered his first shock: a large rat scurrying across a dark corner of the lobby. When he finally settled into a taxi—black with a yellow top—into which the porter had piled his luggage, he discovered that it rattled in a manner that suggested imminent dissolution into its original components. As the taxi lurched into Bombay's populous suburbs, on the road going south to the city, the pavements were lined with squatting people—their backs to the traffic, skinny buttocks exposed, defecating into the road. Then, as the taxi crossed Mahim Creek, beyond which lay the central city, there came into view a mass of tattered hovels, built of splintered wood and straw, with tin roofs. These miserable dwellings were inhabited by thousands of people in an advanced state of malnutrition—the adults dressed in ragged loincloths or saris, the children naked.

Mahim is a tidal creek and, at high tide or during the monsoon season, the hovels were knee-deep in water, so that from them rose a constant stench of mud and sewage. And yet, obviously, the inhabitants had found ingenious ways of making their lives bearable. They had tapped the main electricity lines to provide themselves with free illumination at night and, in some cases, to run the television sets that they had acquired by dubious means. At the edge of the creek there was a slaughterhouse and those whose hovels were nearest it were able, after kicking away vultures and scavenging hawks, to appropriate the offal that the slaughterers had flung down into the creek bed.

A casual traveller today will see none of these things. In the late 1970s the Bombay Municipal Corporation, concerned among other problems with the spectacle presented to arriving tourists, demolished the hovels.

Soliciting alms near a Hindu temple, mendicants extend tin bowls to a worshipper carrying a tray of votive offerings. Begging is an accepted way of life in India, sanctioned by religion, but it has become an embarrassment in Bombay because of the large number of people—more than 50,000—who live in this way.

At the same time the Corporation widened the road from the airport, forbade people to relieve themselves within sight of it and screened off long stretches of it with tin and corrugated iron fences, on which the local children were invited to paint colourful designs. The reservation dividing the widened road carried a carefully spaced line of lollipop-shaped sign-posts, each sponsored by a commercial company and decorated with a brightly coloured Indian bird or flower. On my last visit, the elements had done their work on the wall designs and on the lollipops, so that the road looked like the approach to some decrepit Disneyland.

The cleanliness drive had effects as temporary as the application of cosmetics. Bombay cannot cope with its constantly swelling population. Every day, several hundred people arrive from elsewhere in India in hopes of finding employment. This inexorable influx accelerated during the Second World War when Bombay's industries expanded to meet the demands of the war effort, and tens of thousands of new employees were required by the factories. After Independence in 1947, industrialization continued at a pace that was even more accelerated, since Prime Minister Nehru saw increased industrial production as the future salvation of the country. This policy had staggering effects on the size of the city.

As in any other metropolis of the developing world, the lure of employment in industry draws unskilled workers from rural areas, some to start new urban lives, others to labour as temporary migrants, returning seasonally to their homes. Many come to Bombay not only to find work but because, especially in times of drought and flood, there is nothing but starvation to face in their own villages. Most men come alone, to earn money and send it back to their families; others import their families and increase them in the city. Between 1941 and 1961—a period during which the city's municipal limits were extended to cover most of Salsette—Bombay's population rose by 180 per cent, from 1.5 to 4.2 million; and by 1971 it had reached very nearly six million, approximately half living on Bombay Island and half on Salsette. Since then it has grown by an estimated two million more and, if the present rate of increase continues, it could top 16 million by the end of the century.

More than half the factory employment of Maharashtra State is now generated in Greater Bombay. Manufacturing industries, which range from the cotton mills first established in the 1850s (and still operating 24 hours a day) to pocket-calculator factories set up in the 1970s, provide jobs for about 700,000 people, roughly a third of the city's working population. The rest consists of other manual workers, about 20 per cent; shopkeepers and traders, about 16 per cent; clerical and managerial staff, about 25 per cent; and men and women in the professions, about 6 per cent. Engineering and chemical firms, oil refineries, factories producing electrical equipment, food, edible oil and footwear, and film studios are spread across the central, northern and eastern districts of

Waking in their roadside dormitory near Mahim Creek, rumpled toddlers (top left) sit up beside their sleeping parents, while an early riser sets off with her bedding roll. Bombay's 200,000 homeless have an aptitude for finding rest in public places—even in such unlikely quarters as a heap of coal dust (top right), a stall in the Chor Bazaar (bottom left) and a corner of a shopping arcade near Flora Fountain (bottom right).

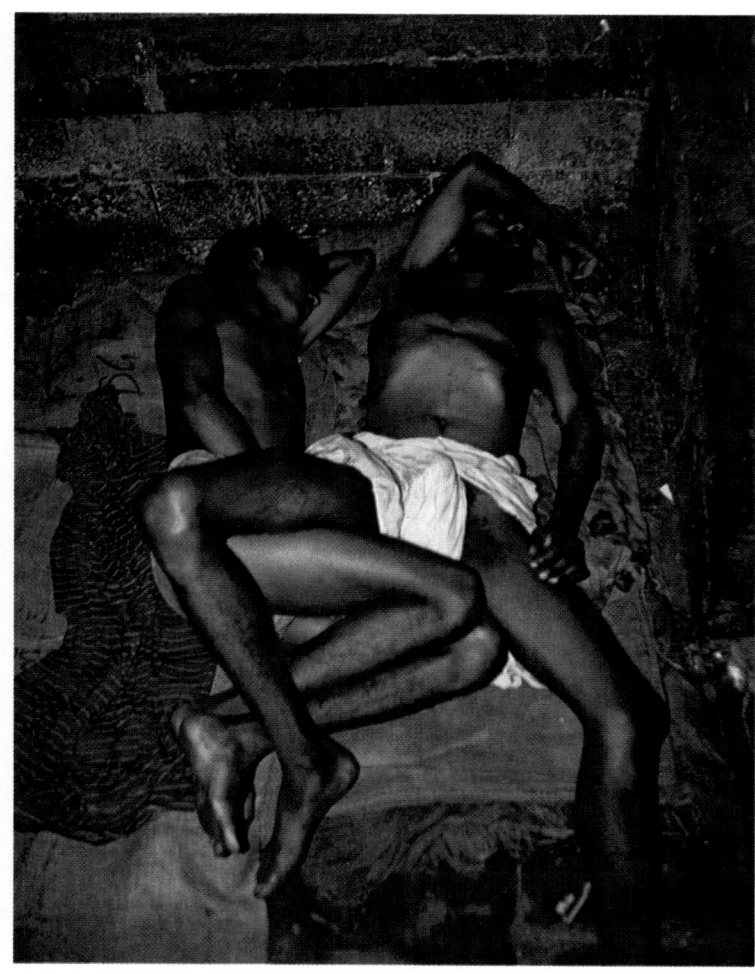

Bombay Island and the suburbs of Salsette to the north. Almost all of the city's textile mills are still concentrated in the area of reclaimed swamp at the centre of Bombay Island, where their belching smoke-stacks contribute to the city's heavy air pollution.

The result of this concentration of industry is the presence of an army of office and factory workers for whom life in the city has meant a substantial improvement in living conditions and security. But for hundreds of thousands of less fortunate people, it means a crammed life in multiplying shanty towns and a daily battle for subsistence. Today nearly three-quarters of Bombay's population live in *chawls* (the city's one-room tenement blocks, originally built for mill workers). A further 15 per cent live in shanty colonies similar to the one that existed in Mahim Creek, where many huts are no more than 10 foot square. At least 2 per cent are permanently homeless and sleep out every night—on pavements, in alley-ways, under porticos; any vacant space is made use of, even the traffic islands in the streets.

Bombay has at least 150 shanty colonies scattered through its industrial districts and suburbs. They lack a proper sewage system and uncollected garbage provides forage for gluttonous goats and ferocious rats. A minority of the people who live in these colonies are relatively well off, holding down jobs that may bring in Rs 500 (about $60) a month or more. They live where they do because no alternative accommodation exists for them. But most of the shanty colonists survive on a bare minimum of basic necessities. They pay a small monthly fee, per hut, to the Municipal Corporation. A casual labourer, earning perhaps Rs 10 to Rs 15 ($1.25 to $2) a day when work is available, cannot afford proper clothing for himself and his family. The shanty-dwellers' main outlay is on food: they eat—once or at most twice a day—plain boiled rice to which has been added a little *dal* (a purée of boiled lentils) and, very rarely, some other kind of vegetable that usually was about to be thrown away by the vendor. When they fall ill, they may resort to one of the dispensaries provided by the Municipal Corporation—although each of these dispensaries may have to cater for as many as 60,000 people.

Many traditionally orientated Indians, however, remain suspicious of Western medical practice and are more likely to visit some local practitioner of folk medicine who, for a rupee or two, sells them a herbal remedy; this may have a real value, or may simply be a placebo—a bottle of coloured liquid or a paperful of powder to be mixed with water. For infectious diseases there are specialist centres; if you break your arm, it can be reset at one of the government-aided hospitals—though you may have to wait in a lengthy queue before this happens.

Above all, there is the insecurity of living in makeshift huts. Money and possessions are easily stolen and families may be attacked by petty criminals. Also, during the monsoon season these flimsy structures are often blown down by the wind or washed away by the rain; and men and women, working knee-deep in mud, frantically set about resurrecting them with bamboo splints, flattened tin cans and tarpaulin rags. There is one minor consolation: the materials necessary for these repairs can either be bought very cheaply or picked up from factory or municipal rubbish dumps.

The city's largest shanty community, known as the Dharavi Labour Camp, just south of Mahim Creek, is inhabited by more than 300,000 squatters; it is said that a new shack is put up there every hour of the day and night. Even in a brief tour of the colony, one can find among its population construction workers, dock-hands, mill workers, truck drivers, domestic servants, hospital staff, petty shopkeepers, semi-skilled workers and junior clerks. Many of these people will have worked their way up from the most precarious beginnings, often being forced to pay bribes in order to get their jobs, as one researcher discovered while doing case studies at Dharavi in the 1970s.

In one of the makeshift huts he found a mill-hand living with his wife and two children. This man had come to the city more than 20 years before

Solidly built concrete roofs protect vehicles on Malabar Hill, one of Bombay's wealthiest residential areas, contrasting with the thatches of straw matting and palm leaves that cover the homes of an adjoining squatters' colony.

from the town of Belgaum 250 miles to the south, and he now earned all of Rs 10 ($1.25) a day. Another man, a truck driver prosperous enough to have acquired gold-capped teeth and a wrist-watch, had travelled to Bombay at the age of 10 from a village in Tamil Nadu State, also in the south. Soon afterwards, he took a job as a waiter, sleeping in the restaurant where he was employed; during afternoon breaks he went to a nearby garage and learnt to be a car mechanic. Eventually he managed to save Rs 300, with which he paid a bribe to obtain his truck driver's licence. By the time he was 27 he could afford to bring back a bride from his native village, but she disliked living in an urban shanty and eventually returned home with their child. He visited her twice a year, when he returned to help his family during the spring and autumn harvest seasons.

One of the few residents of Dharavi who had been born in Bombay was a man whose father had migrated from a village in the Western Ghats, 60 miles away. After being orphaned at the age of 12 he worked as a domestic servant, then pushed a handcart as a street hawker and later became an apprentice mechanic. At the time of the study he was earning Rs 550 a month on the docks as a driver-mechanic for a large food company. To get the job he had had to bribe a company official.

But the life of Bombay's homeless population is even more precarious than that of such relatively established shanty-dwellers. It has been said that if one takes a starting point anywhere in central Bombay and walks 300 yards in any direction, one is sure to run into a colony of pavement-dwellers. For much of the year their alfresco lifestyle is made bearable because it is cooler, in the intense heat, to sleep out of doors. During the monsoon season, however, some of them return temporarily to the villages from which they have migrated; others stay on, finding what cover they can—for instance, under road or railway bridges. On more than one occasion, the Municipal Corporation has resettled pavement-dwellers in dormitory hostels that have been specially built for them in the suburbs. But since these solid brick structures are as much as 20 miles from the city centre, the pavement-dwellers invariably slip out of them and return to slumber in the streets. The great advantage of living on the pavements is that they can be close to their work. Most of them have some kind of regular employment; but others apply for work on a day-to-day basis, turning up in the early morning at the docks or at factories to replace absentees. Many could pay a modest rent if only they could find rooms reasonably close at hand, where they would not have to spend money on commuter fares, and time on travel.

Those who have no jobs beg. A traveller will discover that every time his taxi stops at a traffic-light, he is importuned by beggars, of whom there are several thousand in the city. In Hindu tradition, alms-giving is a meritorious act and beggars therefore have an accepted place in the Bombay community as recipients of charitable offerings. But many of Bombay's

At the start of a long hot day, an ice merchant's employee drags a giant block of ice towards Crawford Market, where it will help to keep fish fresh or cool bottled drinks. Many Bombay restaurants, food shops and drinks stalls lack refrigerators and depend on ice deliveries.

professional beggars, particularly the children, are different: it is alleged that they are controlled by a kind of Mafia, operating in several of the larger cities of India, that acquires small children from parents who can no longer manage to provide for them. Once the children are in the hands of their undesired mentor he methodically prepares them for their calling. He puts a roof over their heads and—shades of *Oliver Twist*—conducts a kind of school for beggars. He teaches them lines of patter, that may differ depending on whether a man or a woman is being approached, a native or a tourist, one who is of average means or one who is visibly affluent. Some are taught how to pick pockets. Dickens' Fagin was mild compared to his modern Bombay counterparts.

A policeman friend of mine explained to me that every morning these children are brought in lorries from the houses where they are kept, usually in the poorer parts of the city or in the suburbs, and scattered in areas that have previously been demarcated by agreement among the various overseers. The children beg non-stop until the lorry comes back, after the places of entertainment—chiefly cinemas—have closed, to pick them up. They hand over their day's proceeds to their particular Fagin, in return for which he feeds them rice and *dal* and a few other vegetables.

There are, of course, true beggars, and in great numbers. Sometimes, poor peasant families, living in surrounding areas of Maharashtra or even further afield, discover that there is not enough food for all if they must also provide for old and incapacitated relatives in their households. In desperation they may bring the old people into Bombay and simply leave them on the streets. The abandoned relatives, helpless, often do not even know where they are. Even if a sympathetic passer-by or a policeman seeks to give them aid, Bombay's overflowing hospitals probably will not be able to admit them: precious medical attention is reserved for those who have a better chance of survival. So these old people beg, while they still have enough strength, probably collecting only enough each day for some rotting fruit or unleavened bread. Even if they could buy rice, they have no method of cooking it.

Then there are the women, often with young children, who were brought from their villages by their husbands and subsequently abandoned. Their intention, at least when they begin, is usually to collect enough money to return home. But they are seldom able to do so. Even if they save money by sleeping on the pavements (where they are subject to sexual attack from young hoodlums), the cost of rice or *dal* or even a little milk for an infant quickly depletes their funds. Furthermore, what little money they do manage to save up is often stolen. Many of the younger women wind up as cheap prostitutes, and malnutrition frequently robs them of their children.

The city authorities have come to regard the beggars as a nuisance and a disgrace. In the 1950s they scooped up the lepers, who were once a common feature of the Bombay pavements, brandishing the speckled stumps of their arms as they appealed for coins, and put them into special asylums or leprosaria. In 1976 the authorities decided to try a similar solution with the beggars. The plan was to give them medical treatment and provide them with work on a dam site a hundred miles inland. Thousands were cleared from the central districts of Bombay, but the plan failed to work. The beggars preferred their squalid but free life on the pavement to country air and the labour that went with it. Soon most of them were back in the city.

In comparison with the precarious lives of the very poor in Bombay, to have a reliable income and live in a *chawl* is to be a person of substance. Most of the *chawls* were built by mill-owners in the late 19th and early 20th Centuries to provide low-rent accommodation for the mill-hands close to their place of work. Such is the shortage of shelter nowadays that as many as 10 people may occupy a single room in a *chawl*, though it is not often that all of them are at home at the same time since the mill workers and other industrial labourers mostly work in shifts. But tens of thousands of clerks and office workers with salaries of perhaps Rs 700 ($90) a month also live in these tenements.

The *chawls* are usually blocks five storeys high and have the benefit of indoor latrines—though each latrine may have to serve upwards of a hundred people and is seldom cleaned. So the tenants queue. They also queue to get water. Some *chawls* do have indoor cold-water taps; but where houses are served by standpipes in the street, one can see in the grey, humid dawn long lines of people carrying buckets, bowls or empty kerosene cans to collect their supply for the day. Because of Bombay's chronic water shortage, these taps are turned on only at certain hours of

A taxi-driver submits to the razor wielded by an itinerant barber. The fee for such a shave is low enough to compare favourably against the capital outlay for a personal razor. For a small extra sum the barber will even perform his duties at the customer's home.

the day and, even then, they often run dry before half the people have had a chance to fill their receptacles.

With so many people to share the modest rent of a room, *chawl*-dwellers are often able to accumulate some savings, especially if their wives also earn wages in a factory. Generally they eat the same staple diet as Bombay's shanty colonists, but they are also able to supplement it. At the end of the day they congregate around the shops and stalls that sell vegetables, fruit, fish or meat. Because of the heat, and the fact that these foodstuffs are seldom kept on ice (which is a luxury), the vendors must sell most of their stock before closing. At that late hour they are prepared to sell, for throwaway prices, fruit that is not entirely sound, fish that is about to turn and items of meat that people with more money will not touch.

Before departing for work, a clerk or office worker from the *chawls* normally eats a slice or two of bread and drinks a cup of tea. At his office, he will buy more tea but this is scarcely enough to sustain him through the day. He cannot afford to spend money on regular restaurant lunches and so, if there is no canteen at his place of work, he will probably bring a packed lunch with him. For the suburban commuter there is another alternative: his meal can be prepared for him at home by his wife, and then delivered to him by an extraordinary meals-on-wheels service.

After preparing the food she will put it into what is called a tiffin-carrier. ("Tiffin", used by the British in India as a synonym for lunch, is in the West usually thought of as an Indian word, whereas in fact it is an English upper-class abbreviation of "tiffing", a verb in common use in England in the 18th Century. "To tiff" meant to take a drink or to have a light meal.)

A tiffin-carrier consists of a set of four small cylindrical boxes made of metal, usually aluminium, so sized that the bottom of one fits neatly into the top of the next. Each box is filled with a different type of food: rice and pickle, for example, are put into one box, *dal* into another, vegetables into the third, and curds in the fourth. The containers are then fitted together into a little tiered column, and the topmost box is sealed with a lid, attached to which is a handle.

After the morning rush hour, a messenger known as a *dabbawalla* ("box man") comes to fetch the tiffin-carrier from the wife. Each man collects from an entire neighbourhood, perhaps an outlying suburb as much as 30 or 40 miles from the Fort area. He takes the tiffin-carriers he has collected to the nearest railway station and places them aboard a train bound for Victoria Terminus or Churchgate Station, with intermediate stops. On the train the tiffin-carriers are sorted and loaded on to trays and trolleys according to destination, for eventual delivery by a second crew of *dabbawallas*.

Around noon, streams of these messengers emerge from the termini—some wheeling trolleys, others with trays precariously balanced on their heads—and scatter over the Fort area. They hardly ever make a mistake: each tiffin-carrier, identical to all the others except for a cryptic code-mark painted on its lid, reaches the man for whom it is intended at about the time he expects it.

Bombay has about 3,000 *dabbawallas*. Because their outlay for rail service is so small, they require less than a rupee a day from each customer in order to manage a modest profit. They have operated their remarkable system for more than half a century.

Kamatipura is the red-light district of Bombay. The whole area, tucked away into the slums north of Grant Road and the bazaars, is itself a sort of bazaar for sex. The brothels of Kamatipura are also known as "the cages" because the windows in the small, filthy buildings that huddle together along the streets are heavily barred. Behind these bars the women parade for passers-by. In the early days of Kamatipura, around the beginning of this century, it may have been that the girls, sold by their parents or kidnapped, were kept in by these barred windows; nowadays the bars exist not because the girls want to get out but because men want to get in; the customers are usually screened by muscular bouncers before they are allowed in. The bars also serve to keep burglars out.

Kamatipura remains as popular as ever, as one might expect in a city that has a thousand men to every 650 or so women. This imbalance arises from the fact that so many men who come to seek work in the city leave their families behind in their villages or are too young or too poor to be married. For an Indian man, getting married is traditionally a lengthy and rather daunting process. Many parents still advertise in the well-filled matrimonial columns of the Bombay newspapers for spouses for their children.

Patient customers accept the ministrations of kan-saf wallas, or professional ear cleaners, working in the Grant Road area (top pictures) and beside a taxi-stand near the Taj Mahal Hotel (below). The charge for this service—a traditional aid to personal hygiene—is about 6 cents. Esteemed for their gentleness and skill, kan-saf wallas use warm mustard oil, a small silver "digging" spoon for the removal of wax, and wisps of cotton for a final clean-up.

These advertisements are couched in a code difficult for the unpractised to understand. I used to puzzle particularly over the frequently advertised "V.V. skilled in H.H.A." until the code was translated for me by a friend. It means "Vegetarian Virgin skilled in House Hold Affairs". If the advertisement is answered, a long correspondence ensues between the parents of the V.V. and her prospective spouse. The couple's horoscopes are compared and eventually a meeting between them is allowed before the marriage is arranged.

Nowadays in Bombay young people are certainly more inclined to participate in the choice of a spouse, but the practical barriers in the way of marriage—poverty and the unequal sex ratio—remain. Today in the relatively affluent and permissive world in which the educated middle class move, college boys may be able to have affairs with young women of their own age and status, or even with a frustrated married woman. Clerks, mill-hands and labourers cannot; they are prevented both by tradition and by lack of opportunity because of their crowded quarters. Instead, they frequent Kamatipura.

The brothels are not illegal; social workers and policewomen inspect them often and are usually friendly with the madam of the house. A policewoman accompanied me to a brothel run by an enormously fat woman with a kind face whose features were almost indistinguishable behind her mask of paint and powder. "When my parents first sold me to a house here," she said, "I was 12. For two years I was taught what I would have to do to please men. At 14 I started. When I was 16 I met *him*." She pointed to a photograph, garlanded and with a stick of incense burning in front of it, of a rather innocent-looking but clearly well-to-do businessman.

"He loved me, so I loved him. Nobody had loved me before. I was reserved for him alone and he visited me every night. I wanted a child by him, but before I met him they had operated on me and I could not have one. Then he died. He left me money without the knowledge of his wife, so I bought this house. It was the only business I knew. The girls usually come to me looking for work; I give them homes here and, if they have children, I see that they are educated."

Generally, in fact, only the male children would be sent to school; the daughters are expected to follow their mothers' profession. I was shown round the rest of the house, which contained the rooms—no more than cubicles smelling of cheap scent and incense—in which the 20 girls of the place lived and worked. Some of the rooms, being in use, were locked. In others, girls were tidying rumpled beds. "They have an average of five or six customers a night," the policewoman explained. The customers pay Rs 8 to Rs 16 (about $1 to $2) apiece. The girls receive their food and keep, a percentage of their earnings and, occasionally, clothes. All of them appeared to be reasonably contented, although those who were mothers complained that, with so many women around, they never had their

Tea-shop service

Speaking in Pictures

The colourful signs and posters that adorn Bombay's buildings may seem naïve to a Western viewer, but often they are shrewdly addressed to the needs, aspirations and anxieties of the native population. Because a significant proportion of citizens are illiterate and the rest divided by language, much of the medium is necessarily pictorial, using images that speak for themselves—for example, the genteel ladies (above) advertising a tea-shop, and the male and female figures (bottom row) pointing the way to the washrooms at Churchgate Station.

Some posters, such as the endorsement for a rat poison (top row, centre), carry a blunt message. Others play upon vague fears, such as the advertisements offering success in mastering "powerful spirits" through self-hypnosis (top row, left) or "spiritual help through magnetism" (middle row, centre), represented by a doctor protecting a cowering patient from a deathly spectre.

A course in self-hypnosis

Pest poison, in English and Hindi

Dairy products, in Marathi

Warning to reckless drivers

Medical protection

Religious goods available

Rest-room for women

"For men"—in English, Marathi and Gujarati

children to themselves. "Also," added one of the mothers, "when we are with a customer and our children are being looked after by a girl who happens to be free, the little ones must have some idea of what we're doing. It's very difficult to bring them up properly."

Kamatipura also offers more expensive brothels; the normal charge in one of these establishments would be about Rs 45 ($6). In a small house, set back from the street, behind gates over which a burly guard kept watch, I was taken into a front room full of girls reading film magazines. The girls were mainly Eurasian or Nepalese and, though not exactly attractive, they were better dressed and made up than those I had already visited. The well-furnished room was presided over by a slim woman in a dark sari, with bitter eyes. "I simply manage this place," she told me. "The owner is a French lady who is asleep at present. She has trained many of our girls in the past, but she is now 85."

Most of the girls in the house, she said, were young widows. All of them lived there in neat rooms with television and private bathrooms. In addition to their cut of the proceeds, they were provided with room and board, free medical treatment and sometimes clothes and make-up. When these girls eventually retire from their profession, some may stay on in the brothel as attendants performing domestic tasks; most of them, however, are likely to return, with the savings they have accumulated, to their home towns or villages. Others may, of course, set up houses of their own.

The over-population so evident in Bombay's *chawls* and shanties is at the root of other evils typical of many Third World cities. It is true that Bombay compares favourably with Calcutta; the population of Calcutta is both larger (by about a million people) and poorer, with daily wage rates only about half those of Bombay. But even so, Bombay's general level of amenities leaves much to be desired. Its problems of hygiene and cleanliness seem insurmountable and appear to breed a fatalistic resignation among officials whose responsibility it is to find solutions. In the last decade the seams of the city have been fraying noticeably. Air pollution has increased with the spread of industry and the rising volume of traffic. Buses and taxis spew out such a quantity of noxious fumes that, from a distance, they appear to be on fire. In most factories, the workers breathe unfiltered air. A Bombay doctor told me that the incidence and variety of respiratory ailments are on the rise even more dramatically than the experts had predicted.

Epidemics, usually of the gastric type, have become prevalent. Deficient hygiene is one obvious cause. Human excrement equally smears the inshore rocks of the beaches and the pavements in the centre of the city. Driving through certain parts of the suburbs, particularly where there are ponds or creeks, the odour is intolerable. Water sources like the Powai, Vihar and Tulsi lakes in Salsette have been polluted by excremental

Pausing outside Bombay's Churchgate Station at noon, dabbawallas prepare for the last stage of the daily operation that brings home-cooked lunches to more than 300,000 office workers. Each food container, known in Hindi as a dabba, is carried by dabbawallas from the client's own outlying dwelling to the nearest railway terminal, then by train to Churchgate or Victoria Terminus, and finally by handcart to his office.

bacteria. There is also, of course, a good deal of putrefaction in the contents of the city's sewers, which normally overflow during the monsoon season. The fly-blown food that is eaten by the very poor is another constant cause of disease.

Bombay at one time prided itself on its hospitals, its doctors and the general availability of medical facilities. In my childhood, I remember being led by my mother or some other member of her family through wards where people lay on clean beds, their eyes alive and hopeful. The doctors called the patients by their names and seemed able to give them confidence. At many of the overburdened municipal hospitals now, one finds a mass of people crouched outside the entrances, awaiting admission. Hospital interiors are often a grid of concrete corridors, lined with sick people (ragged, dirty, some covered by sheets) awaiting beds. The beds themselves are close together and sometimes patients must be laid on the floor in the spaces between. The doctors and nurses appear to be exhausted and few of them know a patient by name, only what disease he is suffering from, and sometimes not even that.

Although most of the drugs and medicaments used are manufactured in India, they are chronically in short supply; this lack of proper medicines poses a constant, intractable hazard. Indian doctors are trained to depend on reasonably modern medicines and equipment. When such facilities are not available, as they frequently are not in Bombay (especially in the outlying suburbs), the doctors may be unable to cope. I was told that what is needed is a powerful corps of paramedics—like the barefoot doctors in China—who would be given intensive training that would equip them to provide basic health treatment not requiring a doctor's attention.

The education system has also shown the effects of the rise in the city's population. The number of schools has increased rapidly, even if the vast majority of them have no playground space. National policy is to provide free and compulsory education for children between the ages of six and 14. The parents pay only for textbooks and decent clothes, although even this obligation is beyond the means of many shanty-dwellers. Nevertheless, Bombay—with its comparatively large municipal budget—has probably gone further than any other Indian city towards reaching the ideal of universal primary education.

For older children, the public educational conditions are far worse. Secondary schooling is the joint responsibility of the Bombay Municipal Corporation and the government of Maharashtra State. Both authorities have agreed that the best language for instruction is a child's mother tongue, so the city's secondary schools teach in all the main local languages. Education of the traditional English sort still continues at select and expensive establishments such as Elphinstone High School, St. Xavier's and at the Anglican Cathedral School—the most fashionable educational institution for the offspring of Bombay's élite, whether

Covered in ash to mark renunciation, an ascetic meditates on one leg. Ropes help him maintain his pose.

Holy Contortionists

Some of the most arresting scenes in the everyday drama of Bombay's streets are provided by *sadhus*, the Hindu holy men who practise self-punishing rituals of asceticism. Although their exotic ordeals draw crowds who contribute alms, the intention is not merely to entertain or make money; unnatural or painful feats of endurance are undertaken as a means of acquiring spiritual power and merit, following an ancient Hindu discipline known as *tapas*. Its adherents include ascetics who have taken vows to stand in one position for years, bury themselves in sand for long periods or even adopt extreme postures that sometimes have the effect of permanently distorting their bodies.

Passers-by gaze at a bedaubed, contorted ascetic and his parrots. The markings indicate he worships the Mahayogi (Great Yogi) Shiva.

In the sand of a Bombay beach, the apparently disembodied hands of a buried sadhu make cryptic gestures. Cracks in the sand serve as breathing holes.

Hindu, Muslim, Parsi or Christian. Furthermore, while it is true that the fees are very low at the government-supported secondary schools, so is the number of teachers, while the number of students in each class is abnormally high. Secondary education begins at 11 and ends at 18, when the student takes the Secondary School Certificate examination, written in his mother tongue. However, many students drop out before completing this phase of their education. The costs of textbooks and supplies escalate at the secondary level; and while the burden on the family increases, so does the potential of teenage children to find work and earn their own living.

On the other hand, only those who pass the S.S.C. exam have some chance of getting semi-skilled, skilled or white-collar jobs. This emphasis on educational qualifications has created a massive expansion not only of secondary schools but college classrooms as well. Between 1951 and 1971, the number of colleges (Bombay has only one university but all colleges are affiliated to it) rose from five to 24. But the student bodies also increased, until overcrowding became so bad that the university governors imposed a limit of 2,500 students for each college. Some institutions thereupon started to run two colleges under different names on a shift system in the same building, one starting as early as 6.30 a.m.

In most cases, pursuit of higher education amounts to preparing for exams by mastering not textbooks, which are too expensive to buy, but guides or cribs to textbooks written by the teachers themselves. The students also attend, at intervals, lectures that are almost always given in English. I was once asked to give such a lecture to students at a new college. The lecture, on modern British poetry, was received in a stunned silence. "Do not worry, sir," said the harassed professor, "hardly any of the students can understand English." I asked what the students did for recreation. "In the evenings," he replied, "they visit the Hindi films;" and then with understandable bitterness he added: "During class hours they wrap pebbles in pieces of inky paper and throw them at me."

Another teacher told me that he had as many bright pupils as in the past but that, because of the overcrowding in the classrooms and the prohibitive prices of most books, standards are falling. Most of the students live hemmed into one or two tenement rooms where the electricity fluctuates, and where parents quarrel and siblings scream—hardly an atmosphere conducive to study. The more diligent are therefore sometimes to be seen sitting on the pavements after dark, perusing their textbooks by the more reliable light of street-lamps.

Because over-population is the source of so many of Bombay's ills, birth control is frequently advocated as the cure. Well-to-do women who devote part of their time to social work have for years been trying to interest their poorer sisters in the less sophisticated methods of family

Framed in first-floor windows (top), bored prostitutes wait for customers in Foras Road, a main street in Bombay's red-light area, while others (below) lounge outside a nearby brothel. An estimated 20,000 girls now serve the vice industry of Bombay, a metropolis in which men outnumber women by a substantial margin.

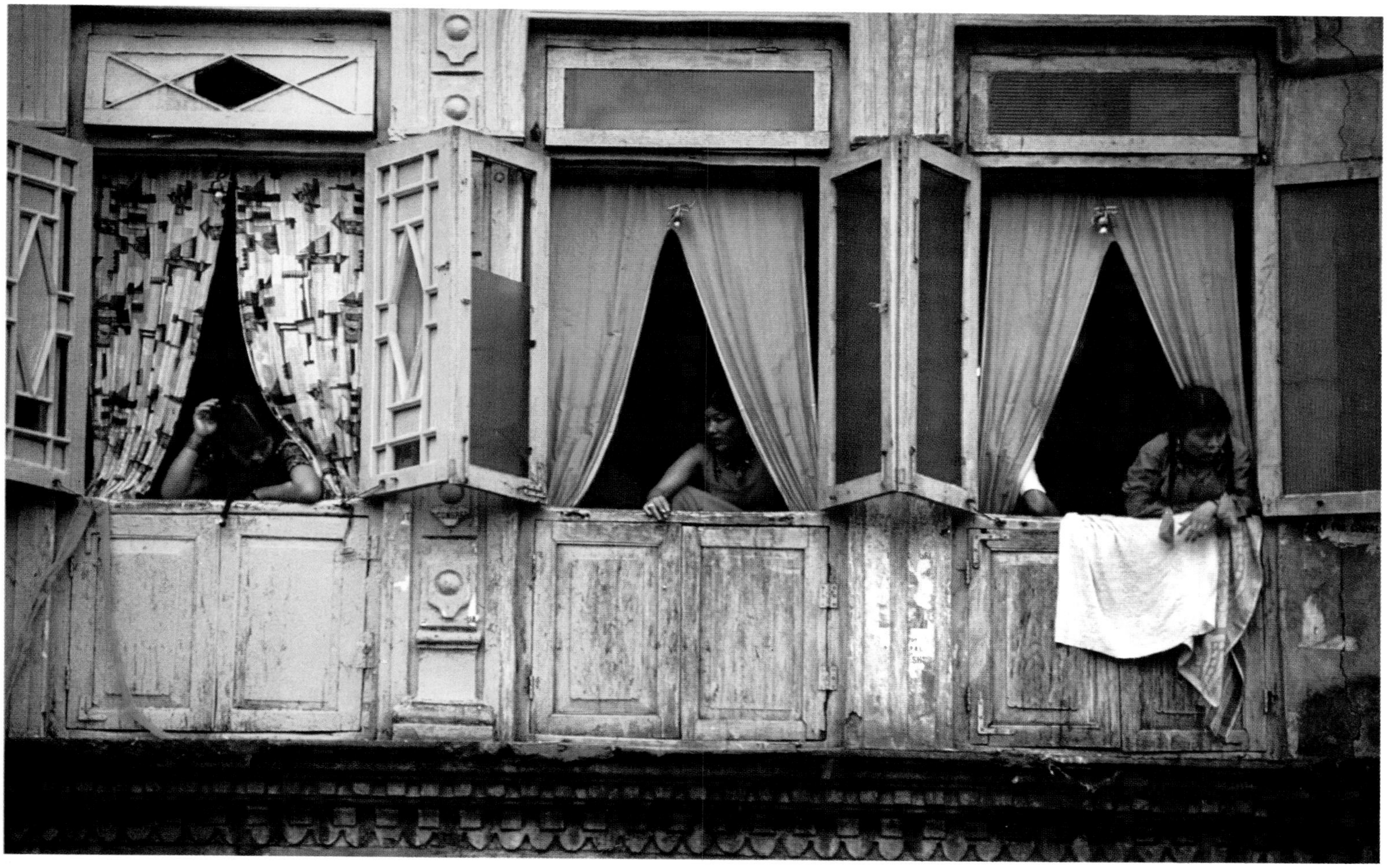

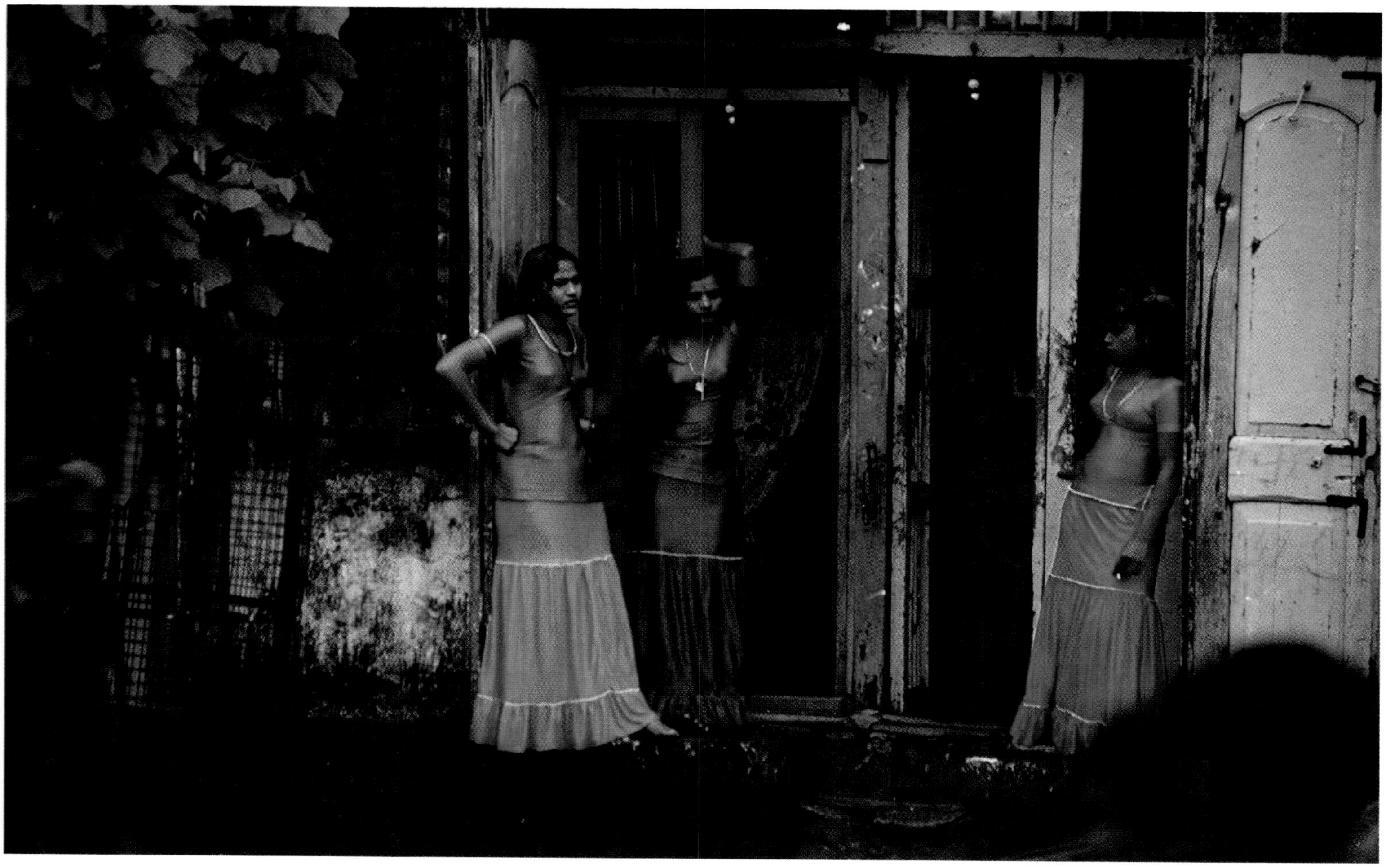

planning. In the early 1960s, shortly after Bombay had become the capital of the state of Maharashtra, it became evident that the growth rate of population was on an accelerating upcurve and might soon become unmanageable. The Maharashtra government then decided to offer people a small sum of money if they would agree to be sterilized. This approach was a small-scale version of the national policy introduced by the Emergency Government in 1975.

The Maharashtrian experiment failed to attract any great number of recruits for sterilization—though the local state government is even said to have toyed with the idea of adding a free transistor radio to the Rs 30 ($3.75) cash sum offered to volunteers. However, at the request of the Municipal Corporation, an enterprising Bombayite, Dr. D. Pai, embarked in 1966 on another campaign in Bombay that, thanks to his unconventional method of publicity, had considerable success. He mounted a family-planning exhibition at a stall in Churchgate Station, where thousands were bound to see it, and furnished it with stacks of hospital admission forms to be filled in by any man who agreed—again, for a small cash reward—to be sterilized. When nobody took the forms, Pai offered to have the vasectomies performed in the station itself, thus demonstrating that the simple operation took no more than three minutes and was safe. He set up a booth on the crowded platform and others at other railway stations; and he also installed kiosks where free condoms were handed out. Soon the booths and kiosks were doing brisk business, as was a fleet of mobile vans equipped with operating tables.

Statistical claims for the campaign must be qualified, however. Many of those who submitted to operations had been enticed by so-called "motivators"—touts who were paid Rs 10 for every customer they brought in; and aged men, very young boys and beggars were among the "volunteers" herded to the clinics by the motivators. But, as Dr. Pai explained to me: "In a war situation—and that's what Bombay's population is engaged in—you have to use whatever means is at hand."

As in all India, the logistical obstacles in the way of implementing a birth-control programme are formidable. There are, in addition, two other impediments: tradition and superstition, both often rural in origin. A farmer needs a family to help him in the fields. And though he may have several daughters, he will want a son to carry on his line and to look after himself and his wife in their old age. After the birth of the desired son the couple may, considering the high rate of infant mortality, want another one as a standby. Also, married couples in villages have been opposed to birth control because they believe it will lead to unfaithfulness; and they have been terrified by the conviction that the sterilization operation causes impotence in men and haemorrhages in women.

In any case, birth control is not the ultimate solution to Bombay's population problem since it ignores the daily influx of migrants into the

A Greek cargo vessel (right) lies at one of the 50 or more berths along the Bombay docks. The port handles more than 40 per cent of India's maritime trade.

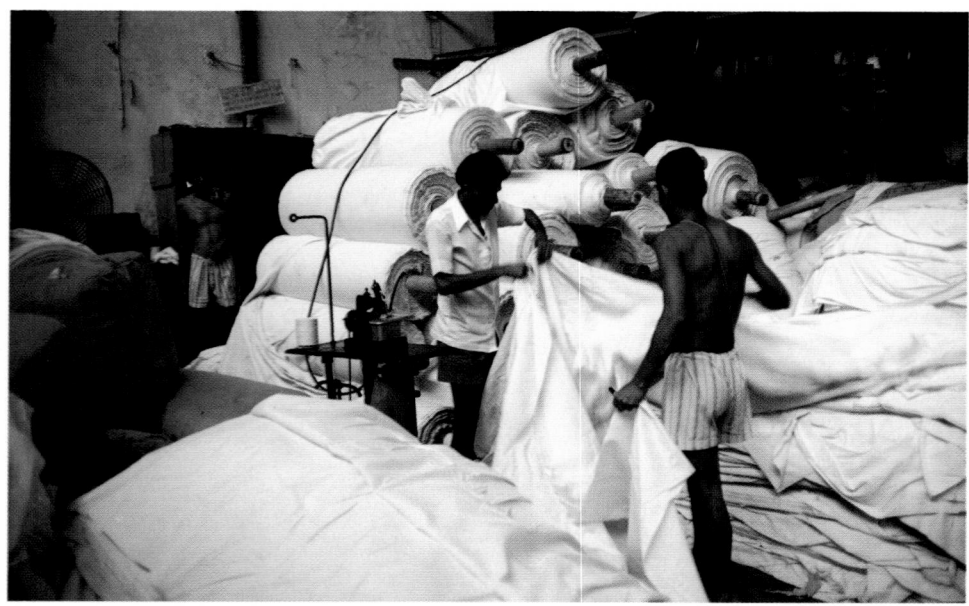

Lightly dressed to cope with the heat, textile workers fold unbleached cloth in a Bombay mill. Cotton manufacture has been the city's main industry since the mid-19th Century and nowadays some 35 per cent of the city's industrial work-force is employed in it.

city. It is a problem faced by many other cities and some extreme solutions have been suggested. In 1974 when I was last in Brasilia, another metropolis with the problem of squatter colonies, there was some talk of erecting a barrier around the city, with guarded gateways through which only people with permits would be allowed to pass. But even if such a solution were feasible for Brasilia, which was planned in the late 1950s and built in an isolated area, it hardly seems possible for a metropolis with Bombay's bulk and sprawl. Building a surrounding wall is impossible and even if every citizen were forced to carry an identity card, and those without one were forced to leave, the police work involved would doubtless precipitate a crime wave in the city.

A more plausible proposal is the creation of a mainland extension of the capital on the eastern side of the harbour. I remember in 1970 standing with my friend Charles Correa, a distinguished Bombay architect, near the Gateway of India. It was the middle of the monsoon season and muddy waves lurched beneath the sea wall. The indistinct outlines of the harbour islands were visible through the drizzle and beyond them the misty mainland—undeveloped territory that offered Bombay additional living space and the opportunity for a fresh beginning. "That's where the new city will be," Charles told me. "New industries can start up there, and we shall put up housing complexes and shopping centres for the workers." I pointed out that numerous workers would by choice continue to live on this side of the water, where all their connections were established. They could hardly be forced to move.

Charles, who with two architect colleagues had proposed this ambitious scheme to the Municipal Corporation as early as 1963, seemed to have it all worked out: "By the time the new city is ready, we will have built a commuter bridge across the harbour. It will have a motorway broad enough to take buses and lorries—transporting industrial products westwards across the harbour to the docks." The Maharashtrian state government, he continued, was interested in the idea, and so were some of Bombay's leading citizens.

"It sounds very ambitious," I said.

"Yes," Charles replied, "it has to be."

On my last visit to Bombay, almost a decade later, I looked out across the harbour from the Taj Mahal Hotel. The bridge Charles had envisioned was still a dream. But the government of Maharashtra State had set up a Development Corporation in 1973 to undertake the plan he had helped to mastermind; some industries and residential housing had indeed been established across the harbour bay; and the latest map of Greater Bombay and its environs now includes an expanse of mainland territory that is labelled "New Bombay". But the energy and imagination that inspired the original planners had collided with an immovable bureaucratic and political lassitude, and—for the time being—everything had come to a standstill.

Meanwhile the pressures on Bombay continue to mount inexorably. Some solutions must soon be found to provide an escape valve, and the creation of a "Twin City"—as the Charles Correa plan is also known—on the eastern side of Bombay Harbour is perhaps the only realistic solution; or at any rate the only realistic one that anybody has propounded so far.

Pavement Emporia

Bazaar traders add an alluring shine to their stock of new, Western-style shoes, envied status symbols in a city where millions wear sandals or go barefoot.

Bombay has more than 70 bazaars: street markets that have a world-wide reputation for the value and variety of their goods. Most of the larger bazaars are crowded together in a city-centre market area, where the different wares are concentrated into specialized sections. Narrow streets flanked by open-fronted shops are filled from end to end with heavily laden stalls, while humbler hawkers—licensed or unlicensed—trade from cloths spread out on the pavement. No matter what the location, the exotic atmosphere of an Indian bazaar changes very little: the seething crowds, the hubbub of dialects, the rich scents that become overwhelming in the inescapable heat. But the array of merchandise—including an ever-increasing selection of factory-made clothing and Western-style articles—provides an informal insight into Bombay's changing way of life.

A salesman awaits customers for brightly coloured, ruffled undergarments.

Glittering headgear can be bought or hired for wear at weddings or festivals.

Using an umbrella as an eye-catching stand, a woman offers a wide choice of inexpensive printed images, featuring Hindu prophets and deities.

A saleswoman's bare feet and traditional costume contrast with her stock of ready-made waistcoats, produced by Bombay's rapidly expanding clothing industry.

A lemon-seller takes a siesta, pillowed on his stock.

Neatly arranged fruits line the walls of a tiny shop.

A well-stocked trader offers various ready-to-eat snacks including puffed rice and assorted chick peas.

Stocking the City's Larder

India has one of the world's most complex cuisines, derived from the country's incomparable variety of produce; the food bazaars of Bombay bring this profusion to the city. Dried staple foods, such as lentils and rice, are easy for retailers to handle, but in a tropical climate fresh produce calls for rapid distribution. Bombay's market area is located just north of the main railway stations, so stalls are stocked daily with fruit and vegetables from the hinterland.

Dozens of varieties of nuts and dried fruits fill plastic bowls and storage jars on the shelves of a dried-foods merchant, known as a farsan walla.

Gathered around a sleeping baby, a group of women gossip on a pavement as they shell a supply of green gram, a type of pea, that they have bought for resale.

Amidst a glowing array of vegetables, traders reach down to serve customers in a covered market, where stalls are tiered to provide maximum display space.

In the aftermath of a monsoon downpour, early evening business continues briskly. Many Bombay bazaars function until after dark every day of the week.

5

In Search of Diversion

At the end of their hot, sticky, noisy working day the ordinary people of Bombay need an escape route, a means of unwinding. The leisure activities they choose are necessarily simple and inexpensive: a game of cards, reading a newspaper, or maybe that ultimate in anodyne entertainment, a visit to a Hindi film. But many Bombayites prefer simply to indulge in *hawa-khana*—that is to say, in a Hindi phrase, "eating the air": to stroll or sit beside the great sighing sea that is so much a part of the city. For one thing, it doesn't charge for the soothing sounds it makes after dusk or for the ozone it exhales, and so a great deal of social activity is centred on it.

Marine Drive, for example, with its rather dilapidated 1930s apartment blocks on one side of the road and the sea wall beyond the pavement on the other, is the city's main promenade. Personally, I dislike walking intensely and normally avoid it. But there was a time in the early 1970s when my wife Leela impolitely observed that I had become exceptionally fat and needed to get some exercise. I therefore tramped up and down Marine Drive twice a day and got to know a good deal about the rituals that are daily enacted there.

In the early morning, men and women who know one another interrupt their beneficial strolls to converse at length about the more recently dead of their contemporaries. They walk there not only for exercise but for social contact, to convince themselves that they are still alive.

In the evenings, after the factories and offices close, the walkers are mostly young people in pairs or in groups. They are always chattering. As a writer I am a natural eavesdropper, but Indians talk so loudly that one does not even need to eavesdrop. Most of the time the conversations centre on culture, or whatever they imagine it to be; and on themselves, which is usual in the young. Small children fly like Cupids towards every couple, trying to sell the boy flowers to present to the girl. They are frequently successful. Pressing the flowers to her nostrils with both delicate hands, the girl may flicker her long eyelashes at the boy in the style of an Indian film star. But she will seldom hold hands with him. Even in relatively Westernized Bombay, it is still not done for unmarried couples to hold hands in public. Two youths may do so; this is accepted—and it does not mean that they are homosexual, simply that they are close friends.

As the young promenaders stroll along the broad pavement, the sea wind sweeps in out of a lurid sunset, ruffling the long hair of the girls, swishing their saris or skirts. The evening traffic rushes by and the lights start to flick on in the apartment blocks across the road. The walkers stop

Before the start of a race at Bombay's Royal Western India Turf Club racecourse, barefoot grooms lead a sleek thoroughbred around the paddock while bettors in the stand look on. The racecourse, the venue of such classic fixtures as the Indian Thousand Guineas and the Indian Derby, attracts about 20,000 people to its weekly meetings held during the racing season, which lasts from November to April.

now and then to sit on the sea wall. They usually sit with their backs to the sea, its glycerine surface sleekly rippled by the tide, and stippled with turquoise and white as the spinning sun drops over the horizon. The spectacle is taken for granted, and so they watch the passers-by and the traffic: the activity of their concrete and macadam environment.

At the north end of Marine Drive, the strollers eventually reach the broad sandy beach of Chowpatty, over which the hump of Malabar Hill rises. Ever since my childhood I have known Chowpatty as a place that is a special attraction at night. Some 10,000 or so people visit it every day to walk, talk, think and—especially—to eat. Food has a particular importance in this city where hunger is an everyday reality; for thousands of Bombayites, eating is necessity and amusement most pleasurably combined. At Chowpatty there are kiosks that sell all sorts of snacks, most notably *bhel puri*. This delicacy seems to have originated in Bombay and is best described as a hollow shell of crisply fried unleavened bread filled with lentils, chopped onions and other vegetables, puffed rice, chutney and spicy condiments—*bhel* simply means mixture. But there are a number of other kinds of *puri*—for example, *pani puri*: small, hollow ovals of light pastry, fried and pierced, then filled with a thin, spicy sauce of which the main ingredient is tamarind water (*pani* means water).

There are also vendors of roasted chick peas dusted with salt and curry powder; and men who, with sharp, curved knives, trepan green coconuts to reveal the depths of liquid within. A transparent water, not milk, fills young coconuts. In my boyhood everyone simply tilted the nut and drank, while the tepid liquid dribbled down one's chin; now the more fastidious customers are provided with straws. When the liquid has been drunk, the shell of the coconut is handed back to the vendor, who scrapes out the white flesh—pulpy or just becoming firm, depending on its age—and offers it to the client. It tastes, not unpleasantly, like slightly rancid dairy cream. In recent years the vendors have developed a new speciality. They hack off the top of the coconut in the normal way, drain off some of the liquid and drop in chunks of ice. The top is then replaced as a seal and, when the coconut is ultimately sold, the liquid is deliciously chilled.

There have been other changes at Chowpatty since my childhood. Once it was merely bare, lion-coloured sand. Hundreds of casuarina, fig and other trees have since been planted and, in addition to the booths of the *puri*-sellers, there are stalls for ice cream, impossibly sweet aerated drinks and sweetmeats. Neon lights are switched on at dusk, and film music blares from loudspeakers.

After nightfall there are also foodstalls throughout the city centre, so that the streets of Bombay smell like a kitchen—though not always a very clean one. Food-hawkers set up shop in little plywood and cardboard kiosks or with glass-topped boxes on wheels that they push around as they cry their wares. Some vendors merely sell sweetmeats—wheel-shaped

A seller of paan in the area of Bhuleshwar, holding a leaf filled to a customer's taste, provides an additional handful of cardamom pods. Prized by the Indians for its fresh taste and digestive properties when chewed, paan consists of the leaf of the betel plant, filled with a mixture of betel nut, lime and spices.

jalebis of fried chick-pea flour batter dripping with sugar syrup, tiny *laddoos* made of the same two ingredients but covered also in melon seeds, and pieces of peanut brittle called *chikkis*. Others sell hot foods: triangular turnovers of spiced minced meat or vegetables called *samosas*; or dishes of fried onions, potato cutlets and hard-boiled eggs, all heavily spiced. Around Mohamedali Road, north of Victoria Terminus, pedlars prepare omelettes and scrambled eggs fortified with mince. Nearby, over *chulas* or small charcoal stoves, other street-traders grill succulent mutton kebabs on long wooden skewers.

I have several times eaten at a kiosk opposite Victoria Terminus run by a quartet of former Indian Army chefs. The speciality there is *pau bhaji*: bread fried in butter and covered with a mass of freshly cooked vegetables, with more butter smeared on top. I have tried the provender of army kitchens all over the world (as a correspondent, not a combatant) and have generally found it unpleasant; but this street snack was not only inexpensive (just one rupee) but excellent.

There is even, just south of Grant Road, a kind of food factory that caters exclusively to people who want *biryani*, for parties or to feed unexpected guests. *Biryani*, originally a Muslim recipe from the north, is a rice dish cooked with lamb or chicken together with onions, potatoes and tomatoes, and flavoured with a rich assortment of nuts, raisins, herbs and spices. Though it is complicated to prepare, the food factory manages to produce it in enormous quantities, cooked in huge vats over wood-fires by men naked to the waist, their sweat-streaked bodies reddened by the demonic flicker of the flames. By Indian standards the cost is rather high—at about Rs 56 ($7) per kilogram (2 lb) of mutton or lamb *biryani*, and Rs 64 ($8) for the same amount of chicken *biryani*. The factory produces at full blast during Muslim festivals.

Unlike *biryani*, few of the street snacks and sweetmeats cost more than Rs 1.50 (18 cents). Nonetheless, they are beyond the reach of the city's poorest people. However, one thing everyone can afford is *paan*, hawked on almost every street and offered for sale for as little as 15 paise (2 cents). The word *paan* means leaf. In this case, it is the heart-shaped leaf of the betel pepper, smeared with various condiments and wrapped round slivers of betel nut, cardamom seeds and other ingredients. (Sometimes tobacco is added.) The resulting triangular envelope is secured with a clove. When chewed, it fulfils roughly the same function as chewing-gum does in America and it is at least as popular, though more disagreeable to onlookers. It fills the mouth with a red, viscous liquid that leaves a tell-tale mark around the lips and is often spat out at intervals against walls or on pavements. Early European travellers to the west coast of India were horrified to notice these red stains and formed the understandable misapprehension, still common among visitors today, that the population was riddled with tuberculosis.

Paan is a breath-freshener and it is also considered to be an aid to digestion. Moreover, its use is not confined to the underprivileged. Formal Indian meals frequently finish with the ceremony of *paan*-making, when the *paan-daan*—a special container for the ingredients—is brought to the table. The ceremony may involve the application to the betel leaf of *vark*, a gossamer-thin layer of edible silver foil, or even of gold foil.

In Bombay's enervating heat, drink is often a priority set above snacks and other refreshments. Around Crawford Market are a number of shops that sell pure fruit juices. The most famous of these outlets is the Badshah, where electric blenders are used to crush the juice from mangoes, pine-apples, grapes and other fruit. A favourite drink is a mixture of sweet lime and orange juices, served with salt, pepper and glucose. At perhaps Rs 2 (25 cents) a glass the price may be a little high for the man in the street, but the quality is high, too. Another kind of drink—if it can be called that, since it is virtually solid—is *falooda*, a preparation based on milk and cream, flavoured with rose syrup, shredded pistachios and almonds, and filled with fragments of transparent vermicelli (the *falooda*). It is coloured pink and looks rather unappetizing, but is so popular that *falooda* parlours are scattered around Bombay, much as ice cream parlours are in many cities in the United States.

Milk mixed with honey and almonds is another favoured drink, especially among athletes. It is the staple breakfast of the *khustiwallas*, or Indian free-

Strollers wander among foodstalls, balloon-sellers and side-shows on Chowpatty Beach. In the background rise the luxury apartment blocks on Malabar Hill.

style wrestlers, who were especially prominent in Bombay in the 1940s and 1950s. They lunch and dine substantially too, so that physically they resemble Japanese sumo wrestling champions. The milk itself used to be obtained for the *khustiwallas* by their managers from what are called *U.P. bhaiyas*, dairymen from Uttar Pradesh, who have come down from their home state in the north of India to make a better living in Bombay; the *bhaiyas* not only deliver milk to private households but sell it in the streets, dispensing it from huge aluminium vats. But the *bhaiyas* have been less in vogue since the establishment of the government-run Aarey Milk Corporation in 1951. The Corporation's vans deliver milk that has been processed and sealed in bottles—and is free from the suspicion of having been adulterated with water. The Parsi Dairy, in the centre of the city, is also notable for the quality of its milk and cream.

Bombay's restaurants are as varied as its mixed population and at midday and in the evening they tend to be full, though they will not be patronized by strongly orthodox Hindus or Muslims, who have scruples about accepting food from the hands of anyone who may be of a different caste or religion. The restaurants are divided by the Bombay Municipal Corporation into three grades.

The Grade A restaurants have air-conditioning and toilet facilities, and are patronized by an upper-crust clientele—bankers, industrialists, judges, film stars—who are accustomed to an air-conditioned world. Restaurants in Grade B, which come within the financial reach of top civil servants, newspaper reporters, small businessmen and other members of the Bombay middle class, have lavatories but no air-conditioning. The majority of the city's restaurants, which fall into Grade C, have neither facility; on the other hand, they offer meals for as little as Rs 2 to Rs 2.50 (25 to 30 cents), and that is what counts to the clerks, teachers and small merchants of the lower middle class, and to the mill-hands and other manual workers out for a rare night on the town.

When I refer to these last establishments as restaurants, I mean that they are places where you can sit down and buy a meal. The cheapest ones usually consist of a single small room—into which the smells and smoke from the kitchen ooze pervasively—with a few rickety tables and chairs, an unshaven proprietor who also collects the cash, and a couple of equally unshaven and slightly less washed waiters who shout at each other and at the cook. They also harry the customers, when the restaurant is busy, continually advising them to eat faster in order to make way for someone else. Indigestion of a chronic kind is thus added to the ailments of Bombay.

Many restaurants trade on a particular speciality, such as seafood—perhaps prawns or the coastal fish called pomfret, which tastes rather like sole and is sold, fried, with chips at fish-bars along Marine Drive and, curiously, at the Marine Drive Aquarium. Two restaurants near Crawford Market and another in the brothel area near Grant Road are known for

On the rocky shore overlooking the Arabian Sea, near the temple of Mahalakshmi, gossiping families enjoy the fresh air. Crowds habitually gather on Bombay's westerly seashores after work, when the heat of the day has subsided.

pigs' feet, or trotters. The trotters may be served in a soup with hot red chilies, stewed without condiments, or simmered in milk. The trotter restaurants are a little too expensive for a clerk, but they are within the means of newspaper reporters and they tend to be much frequented by taxi-drivers, who make a lot of money in Bombay, particularly if they also own their vehicles.

Goan restaurants feature heavily peppered pork and rice cakes; and Sindhi establishments specialize in more mildly spiced meats, especially mutton. Punjabi restaurants, including both branches of the well-known Delhi Darbar, serve long-grain Delhi rice, baked and spiced mutton, sheep or goat's liver and sweetbreads in what is called the *dhaaba* style. This type of cooking is found in inexpensive foodstalls along the main highways in north India and leans heavily on spices and chilies. Vegetarian restaurants, in the main, are run by Gujaratis. The food is served on a large round platter called a *thali*, which may be of silver or some lesser metal. The centre of the platter is piled with boiled rice, and all round the circumference are small metal bowls containing *dal*, curried vegetables, a *farsan* or savoury dish, and some sort of sweet, together with a pile of *puris* or more often of *rotis* (discs of unleavened bread cooked on a griddle).

In the Fort area two distinctive types of restaurants predominate. With the influx of South Indians into Bombay over the last 25 years or so, enterprising cooks from the south-western state of Karnataka have been setting up what are called Udipi restaurants, named after a town north of Mangalore famous for the skills of its cooks—and for their ability to make the maximum quantity of food out of the minimum input. These profitable restaurants serve *dosas*, which are long, tubular rice-flour pancakes filled with spiced potatoes and onions, and *idlis*, cakes made of split peas and rice, eaten with a fiery coconut chutney and with *sambar*, a pepper sauce containing vegetables.

Bombay also has many Irani restaurants, a type of cheap eating-place seldom found elsewhere in India. These establishments are run usually by a single family of Iranians who may be Muslims but are more often Zoroastrians, like the Parsis. (However, because they or their forebears have come to Bombay much more recently than the Parsis—probably not more than a hundred years ago—they still retain their distinctive identity.) Often the peeling walls of their restaurants are adorned with huge portraits of the prophet Zoroaster. Here, for approximately Rs 2 (25 cents), one can eat a bowl of curried mincemeat of dubious provenance, accompanied by a cup of very sweet, milky tea and a slice of buttered Western bread known as "double *roti*" (because it is much thicker than the usually unleavened Indian breads). If a customer is a little more affluent than most, he may be able to indulge in a plate of oily pilaf. All food, whatever its texture, is supposed to be eaten with a teaspoon, the only implement provided. Normally there are admonitory notices all over such premises warning that anyone who steals a teaspoon will be severely punished, and —ever since hippies began to patronize them—that marijuana is to be smoked outside only. I came across one restaurant that clearly had some doubts either about the abilities of its cooks or the digestive powers of its customers, since an ostentatiously displayed placard read: "Do not commit nuisance on floor. Go outside and commit."

For the poor—daily exhausted, daily depressed by the uniform drudgery of work—alcohol has always provided a means of escape. But in Bombay, as all over India, drinking has been fraught with difficulty ever since prohibition laws were introduced after Independence. Years before 1947, Gandhi had been a vigorous advocate of prohibition. Liquor, he said, had serious adverse effects on the lives of the poor; and moreover was not part of Indian tradition.

On this score, Gandhi was only half right. According to the Hindu scriptures, the gods themselves had their divine wine—*soma*; indeed, liquor is mentioned throughout Indian literature; and, from the 16th Century onwards, European travellers returning from India commented on the bibulous nature of the people. The Rajput kings of Jaipur distilled expensive spirits, such as *asha* and *gulab*, which were also available to the rich in many other parts of India. There were several different kinds of *asha*, which had a saffron base: in one, partridges, pheasants and other game birds were sometimes placed in the vat that contained the alcohol and left to liquefy until no trace of them remained except in the richness

Ignored by a small group of idlers relaxing on Chowpatty Beach, a stalwart cut-out figure mounted on a wooden screen advertises the water-skiing opportunities provided by a water-sports club. Boats and canoes may also be hired.

of flavour. The principal ingredient of *gulab* was crushed rose petals. Both spirits were exceptionally potent.

In Bombay at the time of Independence two main kinds of alcoholic beverage were on sale. The more common was a palm wine known as *toddy* (originally *tari*), described by Yule and Burnell in *Hobson-Jobson* as "the fermented sap of the *tar* or palmyra". (Today the sap is usually that of the coconut palm.) The liquid was tapped from the trunk and left in the heat of the sun to ferment. *Toddy* tastes like very sour liquid yeast and nothing like the Scots' "hot toddy"—malt whisky diluted with hot water and flavoured with lemon and spices—to which it has given its name. The other main brew, known as *bevda* and more potent, was made from an assortment of rotten fruits and the coarse brown sugar called *jaggery*.

Total prohibition was enforced in Bombay in 1950 when a teetotaller, Morarji Desai, later to become Prime Minister of India, was law and order minister of Bombay State. The liquor shops were closed down; but in their place numerous speak-easies opened, especially in the suburbs, where most of the stills for bootleg liquor were set up. *Toddy* and *bevda* had certainly provided the drinkers with a terrible crapula the morning after, but this bootleg liquor could cause blindness, madness and occasionally death.

Legal spirits continued to be available in those days, but you had to have a permit to drink them. The permit provided a certain number of units for each month, and each unit was divided into a certain number of points. If you bought a drink in a hotel bar, some of the points (fewer for beer or wine than for spirits) were struck off by the barman and the permit was stamped by a surly excise officer who always sat—a spectral shape—at the end of the bar. To obtain a permit, you had to get a doctor to sign a statement declaring either that you needed one for medicinal purposes or that you were a confirmed alcoholic.

I was in my teens at this time and my father decided that he should teach me how to hold my drink, since I was shortly to leave for studies in England. I therefore needed a permit; but our family doctor, who was opposed to drink and horrified by what my father was doing, refused to sign any statement saying that I was in medicinal need of alcohol. This meant that my only alternative was to be declared a confirmed alcoholic.

My father now sent me to one of the government doctors authorized to issue permits; but before doing so, he handed me a sealed envelope. When the doctor asked me how old I was, said my father, I was to hand him the envelope. An hour later, I confronted a saturnine doctor, who eyed me with suspicion. "You say you are a confirmed alcoholic," he said. "Do you know that means you have to have been an alcoholic for at least ten years? How old are you?" I told him I was 15. "Do not waste my time," he said.

I handed him my father's envelope. He opened it under his desk and I heard a rustling sound. The doctor smiled benevolently at me, placed the envelope in his pocket and said: "So you have been an alcoholic since you

A wall sign, peeling away in a south Bombay street, announces the so-called World Crown wrestling tournament. Although the annual competition in fact draws contestants only from India, the winner is grandiosely dubbed "World Champion". Interest in wrestling has flourished since the 1950s because of India's repeated gold-medal wins in the Commonwealth Games.

were five years old. In a case as serious as this, I will allot you the maximum number of units permissible." He did.

Total prohibition lasted until 1964, when the law on drink began to be relaxed. First, beer could be sold freely, if the shopkeeper managed to obtain a licence. Next, there was no need for foreigners to have permits: they could buy alcohol in licensed shops and they could drink freely in hotel bars. Indians still had to have permits, but points were abolished and licensed drinkers could now consume as much as they wished. Indian companies started to distil alcohol of various kinds (though only the gin and rum are at all drinkable), and the income of the city rose sharply through excise duties and a sales tax on alcoholic beverages.

Further minor modifications to the law on drink have since taken place and will continue to do so, for prohibition in India remains a live issue. Meanwhile illicit stills and speak-easies continue to operate in the poorer suburbs of Bombay, offering alcoholic beverages at prices far lower than those for officially approved spirits. For the middle class, there are now bars all over the city and they also offer food along with spirits. A typical example is Pyrke's near Flora Fountain—formerly the Provision Stores where my mother used to shop, and today, under different management, a popular drinking-place. A gin and tonic at Pyrke's, as at other such places, will cost around Rs 4 (50 cents), compared with about Rs 16 ($2) at the Taj Mahal Hotel. With it come nuts, slivers of Bombay duck and potato chips. However, the waiters may be dirty and rude; the food, if you eat while you drink, is slapped down on the napkinless table, showering the customers with greasy rice and bits of fish or meat. Establishments such as this, patronized by the city's fairly well-paid writers, artists and bureaucrats, are, in their way, equivalents of the few London pubs still allowed by the brewery landlords to maintain a kind of individuality, or of the cheapest bars in New York City. Similar places exist in Calcutta, but not in Delhi or Madras.

Bombay has always been a place where athletes have been heroes. In sport, rich and poor share a common enthusiasm. Soccer and field hockey are especially popular in the city and so, too, in its gentler way, is badminton. But leaving them far behind is cricket. Almost all parks of any size—especially the Maidans in the Fort area—are packed, during holidays, with schoolboys playing the game, the pitches sometimes so close together that the fielders in one match intermingle with those in the next. Whenever India is playing in a Test, or international, match, Bombay echoes to the chirp and crackle of cheap transistor radios clutched to the ears of half the population. If the Test is played in Bombay—there are three Test grounds, the Brabourne and the newer Wankhede Stadium, both off Marine Drive, and the Bombay Gymkhana, adjoining the Azad Maidan—the business of the city is further impeded: on the day when the match starts half the employees report that a close relative is ill or has suddenly perished; and the protracted funerary rites always seem to take five days—the exact duration of the Test.

All the schools and colleges in Bombay have cricket teams and, at the city's communal gymkhanas along Marine Drive, the sons of well-to-do Hindu, Muslim, Parsi and Catholic families have the chance to compete against men who have represented India in Test cricket. When matches are played on the grounds of the gymkhanas, all classes are united, though across a gulf of grass and money: while the rich watch the game from well-appointed club-houses, the ordinary citizens of Bombay do so from Marine Drive. Between 1958 and 1974 the standard of cricket in Bombay was so high that the local Bombay team won the main all-India tournament prize, the Ranji Trophy, in every single year; and several of India's foremost cricketers come from Bombay.

Curiously enough, the cricket history of Bombay illustrates the tolerance that prevails among the city's different communities. In 1882 the British started to play annual cricket matches against the Westernized Parsis. In 1907 the Hindus came into the picture, and in 1912 so did the Muslims, so that a four-way tournament known as the Quadrangular was created with players drawn from all over India. In 1937 a fifth team, the Rest, was formed. It consisted of Christians, Sikhs and members of other communities, including visiting players from Ceylon. The tournament then became known as the Pentangular. At Brabourne Stadium, where the matches were held, each gymkhana had its own stand, from which spectators cheered the players of their own community. Despite the

Club members relax on the terrace of the elegant Royal Western India Turf Club. Founded in 1800, the club is one of Bombay's most fashionable meeting-places.

emphasis of these matches on separate communities, however, the players were friendly both on and off the field; and the spectators, if often excessively noisy, were not in conflict with one another.

In the mid-1940s, Gandhi—who was not, so far as is known, a cricket enthusiast—took an interest in the tournament. He insisted that a competition which split up its participants on a communal basis was not in the interests of national unity and should be stopped. It was, in fact, stopped in 1946; and though a roar of protest went up all over India, Bombay, the home of the tournament, acquiesced.

The wealthy of Bombay enjoy their expensive pleasures in a world apart from the city of sweaty crowds, smelly restaurants, illicit stills and cheap foodstalls. Bombay has more wealthy, Westernized people than any other city on the subcontinent; and in matters of fashion and entertainment, they set the trend for the whole of India. The permissive, whisky-and-soda lives of the rich, projected in type-cast imagery through the city's Hindi films and through Bombay's advertising industry, the largest in the country, are of absorbing interest to the whole population.

On the highest stratum of society, represented by the families of executives and industrialists, there are certain fixed areas of entertainment. Cocktail parties are the main recreation; almost invariably they are formal occasions to which, for reasons of prestige that have persisted since British times, a quota of foreign diplomats and businessmen is invited.

At these parties foreign liquor (a bottle of good Scotch costs about $50 in Bombay) is usually served; and if the cocktails trickle on into the dinner hour, there is a buffet of mixed Western and Indian, and sometimes Chinese, food. Brandy follows. The men wear dark suits and talk about business, the stock market and politics, segregating themselves from the women. Their wives, aromatic and svelte, mostly wear low-cut, backless *cholis* and hipster saris; their talk generally centres on art, literature and social work. Many of them belong to clubs that hold concerts and raffles to raise money for charity. Some teach part-time in schools for poor children; others collect clothes and toys to be sent to such schools.

If she has children, the wife does not have to look after them; either they are in the charge of servants or else they have been consigned, in smart school uniforms, to be educated at superior private teaching establishments. At the weekend the whole family may drive with the children and *ayah* to the beach-house which they or the husband's company own, whether at Juhu or Versova, Manori or Marve. They picnic, swim, walk, sleep, eat and enjoy the sensation of inhaling the sea air—though it may sometimes smell of dead fish. But the weekdays are often insoluble for the wife: the evening may promise a cocktail or dinner party, but the day— glaring with sunlight in summer, blind with rain in the monsoon season —consists, like her children's jigsaw puzzles, of pieces that she must fit

Neatly dressed in white—almost a uniform in Indian schools—children pore over their sketch-pads at a drawing competition organized by a local charity on the Oval in the Fort area of Bombay. Education is free and compulsory for all between the ages of six and 14, but only about two-thirds of Bombay's children persist beyond 11; those from poorer families usually drop out in order to become wage-earners.

together herself. She may fill in her time by playing cards with other wives, for highish stakes; or, not unnaturally, acquire a lover. The incidence of adultery in Bombay, among the rich, is probably no higher than in any other large city; but it is a relatively new development, as Bombay has followed the fashion of the permissive Sixties in the West.

When, during the season, there are races at Mahalakshmi, she perches like some bright bird amidst an aviary of her kind, breasts fluttering under her *choli*, watching through binoculars purchased overseas as the horses thunder round the track. She places small bets and giggles when she wins, for this at last is fun. Opposite the club-house, on the road beyond the race-track, are a huddled multitude of working-class people. They are more anxious than she is about their own modest bets, but enjoy the spectacle perhaps more than she does: the green turf, the splendid thoroughbreds, the vividly arrayed jockeys, and the crowded, clapping, colourful grandstand.

Another area of entertainment for the wealthy is the hermetically sealed ambience of the expensive hotels, especially the two most expensive of all, the Oberoi and the Taj Mahal. The Oberoi is much like any other new skyscraper-type hotel, and the old Taj—the splendid, the historic Taj, inextricably linked to its new Inter-Continental wing—has become, like the rest of Bombay, a weird mixture of an old and dignified world and a new brash one. Guests with some thought of history prefer to stay in the old wing, populated by its ghosts of suicides who, driven by unrequited love or financial ruin, leapt down the immense stairwell; or of British officers wiping whisky off their moustaches as they sat under the grinding, wheezing electric fans and surveyed the island-haunted sea from their eastward-facing suites.

At the old Taj, regular customers faithfully make their way to the hotel as part of their daily routine. Some, in fact, breakfast there every day. To descend from the old-world courtesy, shadows and whispers of the original Taj and, as soon as you pass the Harbour Bar, find yourself in the new wing of the hotel—the marble lobby full of Arabs and tourist parties, with pretty wenches in hipster saris behind the desk—can be a traumatic experience.

The Rendezvous restaurant in the old Taj, where I ate with my father in the 1950s, has been swirled up to the top floor of the Inter-Continental wing, where it has become a D-shaped room with the outer curve facing the harbour. The Rendezvous offers the only authentic French food in town; and you can even drink French wines, though the better vintages do not travel well and the prices are very high. On the ground floor the Golden Dragon, the hotel's Chinese restaurant beside the Harbour Bar, serves Szechwanese food of fairly good quality; and the Tanjore restaurant, which serves south Indian food, is excellent of its kind. The Taj's own discothèque, the Blow-Up, is in sharp contrast to the rest of the hotel.

At Bombay's Stock Exchange on Dalal Street bidding among brokers—almost all of whom come from Bombay's Gujarati and Marwari communities—has the appearance of a frenzied altercation. Founded in 1875, the association is the oldest of India's eight stock exchanges.

Here are to be found psychedelic lights, an immense amount of noise and the offspring of the rich in considerable numbers.

The younger generation of wealthy executives often live a double life. Though they may wish to be completely Westernized, their parents and older relatives frequently disapprove of their lifestyle. During religious festivals or on family occasions when the generations are expected to mix and meet, the younger couples are probably rather startled to be reminded of how Indian they are. On the other hand, the rich who still live in a joint-family system that enforces certain taboos at home, who cannot eat meat or drink alcohol when their grandparents are around, suffer a cultural shock when they have to deal with foreign clients or friends.

The Kilachand family, one of the richest in Bombay, live according to this joint-family system in one of the last great Parsi houses in the city, on Nepean Sea Road near Malabar Hill. The house was built by the Dubash family in the 1890s, sold to the Maharajah of Patiala, a Sikh, and in turn sold by him to the Kilachands, who are Jains. It is approached through great gates, up a long curve of gravelled drive. Invited there one evening for drinks, I saw it first as a ghostly white bulk, spectrally lit, like a ship afloat amidst an ocean of lawn. I ascended a flight of stairs to the first floor and entered a gigantic, high-ceilinged drawing-room fronted by a broad verandah. Almost the whole Kilachand family live in the house: the grandparents, their children (who included my host), and the children's families: 24 people in all. Each family inhabits its own self-contained suite, which is luxuriously furnished.

A wealthy Parsi industrialist chats with guests in the roof garden on top of his office building, a prime site overlooking the open space of the Azad Maidan.

I sat down with Mr. Kilachand and his pretty young wife, and sipped a soft drink, which was all that could be served since I had arrived on a Jain holy day. Glancing around the huge room, I inquired how many servants it took to look after 24 people. "Thirty," said Mr. Kilachand, a modern young man, somewhat apologetically. "You see, the children have to have their *ayahs* and in a house this size we have to employ a lot of watchmen and gardeners." I asked if he didn't find it rather overwhelming to live in such a big house, even if the other inhabitants were members of the family. "Ask my wife," said Mr. Kilachand.

She said, "I've been going on about that for years. One has no privacy here. Also, you have the feeling that your children don't belong to you. They are always with the other children, and all the children are thought of as the property of the whole family. I want to feel my children are my own. That, basically, is why I have been asking my husband to move us into one of the flats we own in the city."

Apart from the Westernized and the more traditional rich families, there is a third very distinctive group of the affluent in Bombay, new since the Second World War—particularly those who have made their money in advertising. Brought up in a Western way and educated abroad, they are hybrids. They long for the culture they left behind in their student days, and so they attempt to recreate these conditions in Bombay. They attend film clubs that show films from abroad or else New-Wave Indian films that lack the mass-market appeal of the typical Hindi movie and will never reach the commercial circuits. After a show, they collect at the flat inhabited by one or other of them; there they drink coffee, play loud pop music, and sometimes smoke marijuana. The men wear Indian *kurtas* and pyjamas—loose clothes made of handwoven cotton, but tailored; their hair is long, but trimmed and blow-dried. The women dress either in kaftans or in low-slung saris. All become intense in their discussions of the film they have seen, or perhaps of the latest play—it will be a Western play—produced at the amateur theatrical club to which they belong.

For a cultural life to develop, a city needs galleries, museums and libraries; and, around these, small shops where people can buy books and records at reasonable prices. In Bombay, such an infrastructure exists, up to a point. There are museums like the Prince of Wales, with its three main sections devoted to art, archaeology and natural history; and the smaller Victoria and Albert at Byculla, the oldest in Bombay, with its natural history, geology and agricultural displays. Apart from the prestigious Royal Asiatic Society Library (open only to members), there are about a hundred libraries attached to colleges and institutions of higher learning, and about the same number of subscription or public libraries, though these are poorly stocked. There are several art galleries, of which the biggest is the Jehangir, opened in 1952. This gallery has various annexes, including a popular downstairs restaurant called the Samovar where intellectuals and those with intellectual pretensions are apt to gather. The atmosphere smacks just a little of an indigenous Les Deux Magots, the Left Bank café in Paris that earned a similar reputation before the Second World War.

Pavement bookstalls abound in Bombay, thriving mainly on the works of such pot-boiler writers as Harold Robbins and Barbara Cartland in paperback. Even these are expensive for a young person, costing perhaps Rs 16 ($2) apiece. There are also numerous bookshops in more imposing premises, where the prices for paperbacks are even higher than they are at the wayside stands. But the older bookshops may contain unexpected treasures for solvent older readers.

At the back of Taraporevala's, a Parsi bookshop off what was once Hornby Road and is now Dadabhai Naoroji Road, a dusty back room contains shelf upon disarrayed shelf of books of all kinds. Had one the time and patience to sift through its stock, it is possible that one might turn up valuable first editions, though they would probably be in poor shape.

In the district of Kalbadevi, beyond Crawford Market, my father and I in the 1940s used to rummage through little shops where there were old books, often the entire libraries of Englishmen who had sold them off before moving back to Britain. Curiously, these collections were sold by weight rather than individually according to their value. Even in the early 1950s one could find in such shops very rare books on India, with hand-coloured illustrations mounted in them, and dried tobacco leaves placed between occasional pages to keep the white ants away. There were first editions of Dickens, Scott, Thackeray and Trollope, thumbed by tired Englishmen and women in up-country stations—monuments to their boredom. Now, of course, it is much more difficult to find such things.

A number of shops in the centre of Bombay sell records, mostly current Western hits, but also Indian classical music. The young of all communities are interested in Western pop music, but also—since some of the world's more serious pop musicians have declared an interest in traditional Indian music—in the indigenous classics. Western classical music is much favoured by the Parsis, who often sponsor concerts by orchestras from Europe and the United States. But few intellectual entertainments are within the reach of a poor young man or woman. For them, the city has failed to provide any artistic outlet.

Men of good will have plans to bring library facilities, theatre productions and concerts within the reach of a wider cross-section of the population, and one day, perhaps, many more people will be able to participate in the city's cultural life. It is all a question of money—and time. Meanwhile a trend towards a democratic sharing of less cultural pleasures can already be discerned. An example of what I mean is the change that has come over Juhu Beach, 12 miles from the city centre near Santa Cruz Airport. Juhu is a long sweeping curve of yellow sand on which waves of innocuous appearance continually break; but despite the gentle invitations of the sea, few people swim at any distance from the shore because there is a treacherous undertow that, over the years, has claimed a number of victims including relatives of mine and of my wife.

In my childhood Juhu was a rather secluded, exclusive place. I remember as a small boy spending a particular Sunday there with my parents. After nightfall I walked up the beach alone. There was nothing else alive there except for the tiny crabs whose burrows showed like bubbles in the sand; they were a dusty colour, each the size of my fingernail. The night sky was full of cold, flinty stars; the coconut palms creaked in the wind like the masts of a ship; and though the tide had receded I could hear, far away, the susurrations of the sea and the occasional dull crash of a wave. My nostrils were full of the iodine odour of seaweed, the cold musty smell of the rocks and, blown in from the dark distance, the smell of the sea itself, huge and implacable. Some curious instinct told me that it was not I who watched the sea and the stars, but they that watched me.

Such Wordsworthian concepts would hardly be possible to a child at Juhu today. The place has lost the loneliness which, for me at any rate, was its essence. Weekend cottages and a few more regularly occupied houses (some belonging to Indian film stars) are no longer the only buildings nestling among the coconut palms at the fringes of the beach. Multi-storey hotels now loom large. Lining the sea front, as at Chowpatty, are brightly painted stalls that sell ice cream and cold drinks and snacks, not to mention souvenir dolls concocted of sea shells, glue and wire. Thousands of week-end trippers leave their debris behind, and the shifts of sand and sea are the only methods of rubbish disposal. There are entertainments for children—rides on camels, ponies and donkeys—and adults can, if they wish, hire horses.

So little exists in the way of amusements for the Bombay masses that I cannot bring myself to blame anyone for the recent intrusions on this beautiful and dangerous beach. If there is blame, it belongs to the congested city, of which Juhu happens to be a part.

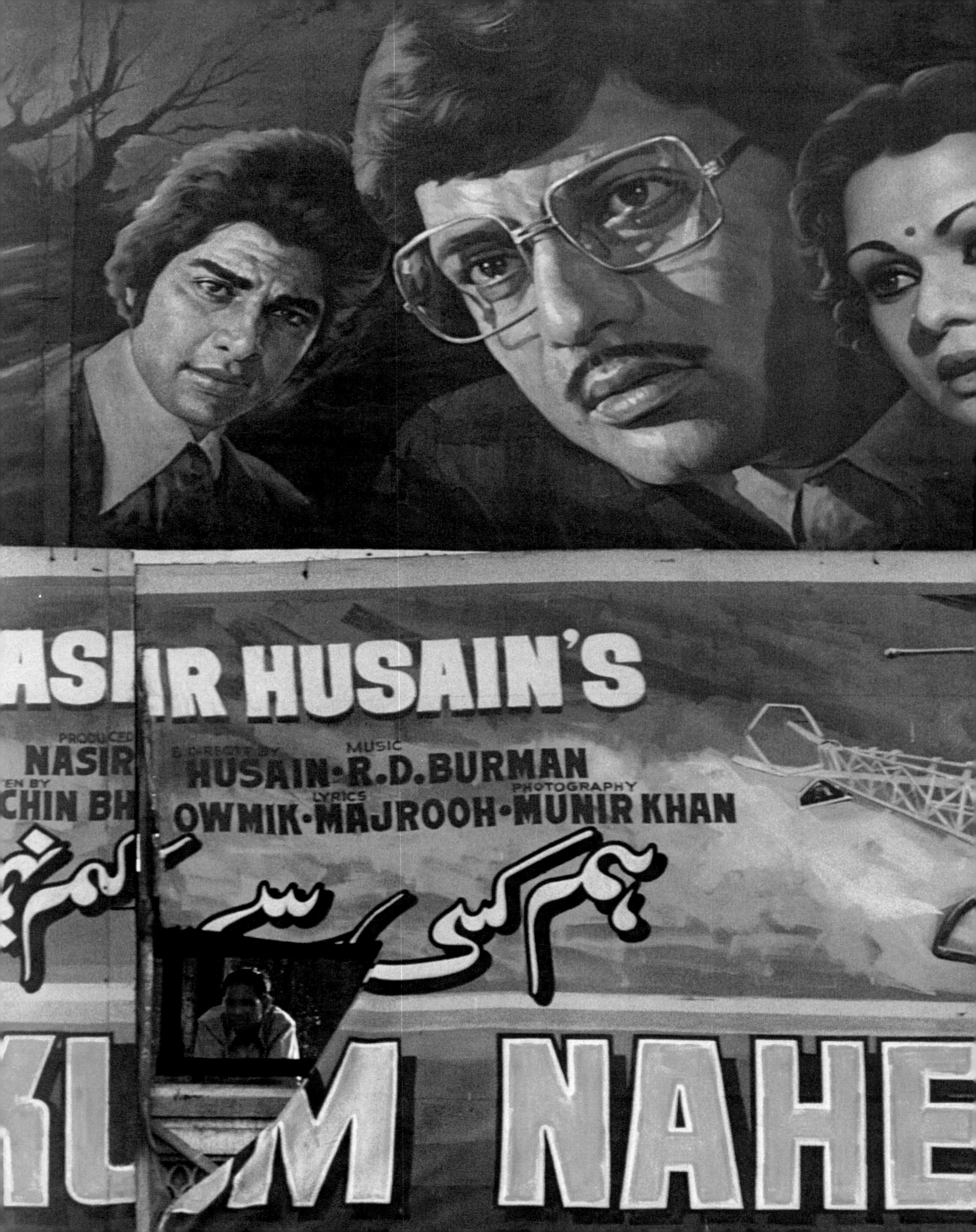

ASIR HUSAIN'S
PRODUCED
NASIR
MUSIC
HUSAIN · R.D. BURMAN
LYRICS
PHOTOGRAPHY
CHIN BH
OWMIK · MAJROOH · MUNIR KHAN
ہم کسی سے
NAHE

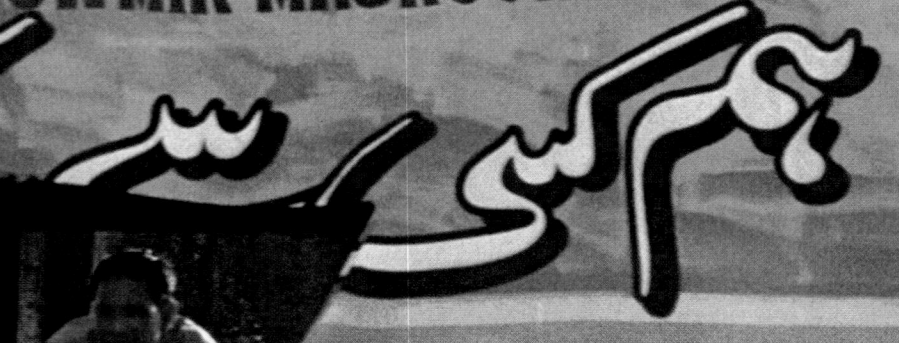

6

The Dream Manufacturers

Since the 1950s, the Indian film industry has been the biggest in the world; and some 30 per cent of its production comes from studios located in Bombay, which has often been called the Hollywood of India. Pali Hill in Bandra, north of Mahim Creek—where many of the top stars, amongst the most conspicuous of Bombay's rich, have their luxurious homes— could be called the Beverly Hills of Bombay.

The city's film industry was established a very short while after its inception in Europe. In December 1895 the Lumière brothers opened a cinematograph in a Paris restaurant; seven months later, on July 7, 1896, the first film was shown in Bombay, at Watson's Hotel. An Indian named Harischandra Bhatvadekar (better known by his affectionate nickname Save Dada) saw the commercial possibilities and ordered a movie camera from London, with which he filmed a wrestling match in Bombay. It was the first film ever made by an Indian, though it had to be processed in London. He also made some news-reels before acquiring a projector with which to show his own and imported movies. From the titles of the time—*Train Arriving at Bombay*, for example—it clearly was not what the audience saw that mattered but the fact that they saw it at all. However, in 1909, R. G. Torney, a member of a dramatic club in Bombay, directed and shot a popular Marathi play called *Pundalik*. The film was simply a visual record of one performance, but it can be called the first feature film shot in India. Other early entrepreneurs put on travelling film shows, which went through such rural areas as were accessible by road, pitching a tent in each village, setting up a screen before a peasant audience and introducing the incredible to the incredulous.

One of the pioneer distributors was D. G. Phalke, who hauled his screen, projector and reels around India by bullock-cart. Phalke was a man of prodigious talent, the "father of Indian cinema", after whom a film award as well as a Bombay street are named. In 1912, using his skill in trick camerawork, he made a movie called *The Growth of a Plant*. It showed the germination and growth of an ordinary pea plant, but it was the birth of the Indian cinema. From the profits, Phalke was able, a year later, to finance his first full-length film, *Raja Harischandra*—a 50-minute epic about a Hindu king. Its enormous success coincided with the conversion of many of Bombay's old legitimate theatres into cinemas. By the time King George V visited Bombay, at the end of 1911, rival news-reel companies were engaged in fierce competition. One company, Excelsior Cinematograph, scooped its competitors by hiring a special tramcar to

His view obstructed by a giant billboard that advertises a Hindi film, the top-storey resident of a Bombay apartment block has solved the problem by tearing out a section of the poster. Bombay is a thriving centre of production for Indian films; the city's numerous studios churn out more than 150 movies each year for keen cinema-goers across the subcontinent.

follow the royal procession. Two trained operators brought from London printed the pictures in three and a half hours, using 3,000 pounds of ice to keep down the temperature in the processing room.

By the start of the First World War a number of Indian films were being made each year and shown, mostly in Bombay; and many movies were also being imported from Europe and the U.S.A. Those produced in India were mainly based on myths, or on social satire, of which a favourite theme was the affected Indian who had returned home from an English education. (Early on, all films were placed in three categories: mythological, historical or social; they are still—somewhat anachronistically—classified that way today, although movies in the social category now far outnumber those in the other two.)

The situation became more complex in 1927, when the era of the talkies began. The new necessity for making films with dialogue in an Indian language afforded a certain degree of protection from the competition presented by imported foreign films, but there were so many different languages in India that it was clearly impossible to make movies in all of them. The Indian industry was thus fragmented into different centres, of which Bombay, Madras and Calcutta were—and are—the most important. For the same reasons that made Hindi the official language of unified India after Independence, it soon became obvious that the bulk of films made in India would have to be Hindi, the language that was most widely spoken and understood. Furthermore, Bombay, where the film industry had started, already had more facilities—in terms of studios, trained technicians, theatres and equipment—than any other city. Bombay thus automatically became the first centre for the national film industry and has remained the home of Hindi movies ever since. Today, Madras—producing films in many of the languages of southern India, including Tamil, Telugu, Kannada and Malayalam—far outdoes Bombay in quantity, completing about twice as many movies. (Calcutta, on the other hand, devoting itself chiefly to Bengali films, may make one-third as many as Bombay.) But the largest number of feature films in any one language—nearly a third of the country's annual total of perhaps 600 movies—still comes from the Hindi studios of Bombay.

It may seem curious that a country as poor as India should produce more films than any other country. But with 75 million people going to the movies every week, India has the largest audience in the world—an audience that in the cities pays a typical cinema admission fee of Rs 1 to Rs 3.50 (12 to 44 cents), and that has no real alternative entertainment to tempt it away. Television—government-run and still largely used for educational and informational purposes—does not begin to compete with the cinema for the speculative investment of private enterprise, while the rewards to be gained from films distributed on such a vast scale are

Before work begins on a new film, producer, director, camera crew and leading actors gather around a sacred fire on the set. The auspicious date for this Hindu ceremony—a muhurat—has been ordained by an astrologer. After Sanskrit verses have been read, a brief sequence of the film is shot to ensure the venture's success.

correspondingly impressive. One successful movie earned nearly $2 million in just 6 months after release in only three big cities.

The rewards for the government, by way of tax revenues, are significant too—about $150 million a year. Exports add perhaps $10 million annually in foreign exchange. Although they contribute only a small proportion of such earnings, the classic works of renowned directors such as Satyajit Ray and those of a generation of younger directors—including such names as Kumar Shahani, Mani Kaul and Shyam Benegal—have won for India international respect. The national government involves itself considerably in the industry. Most documentary films and news-reels are made by the government; cinema licensing regulations require that one or the other be shown with every commercial feature. To promote high quality, a government-sponsored Film and Television Institute was started in 1960 at Poona on the mainland opposite Bombay. The Institute's extensive library includes both films and film .literature. Prospective students who wish to act in films, or to produce or direct them, are screened by a selection committee consisting of actors and producers; but for cameramen and technicians the only qualification is a Bachelor of Science degree. Fees are paid except by those students who gain admittance to the Institute on a scholarship.

Also in 1960 the government set up the Film Finance Corporation to underwrite "films of high quality and good standard". There is, in addition, effective encouragement from the various state governments for local language films.

But the typical Hindi films churned out by the commercial studios of Bombay are something quite different from the critical and creative

On an opulent set in the studios of Raj Kapoor, one of Bombay's foremost film-makers, a camera crew shoots two Indian stars emoting in a seduction scene.

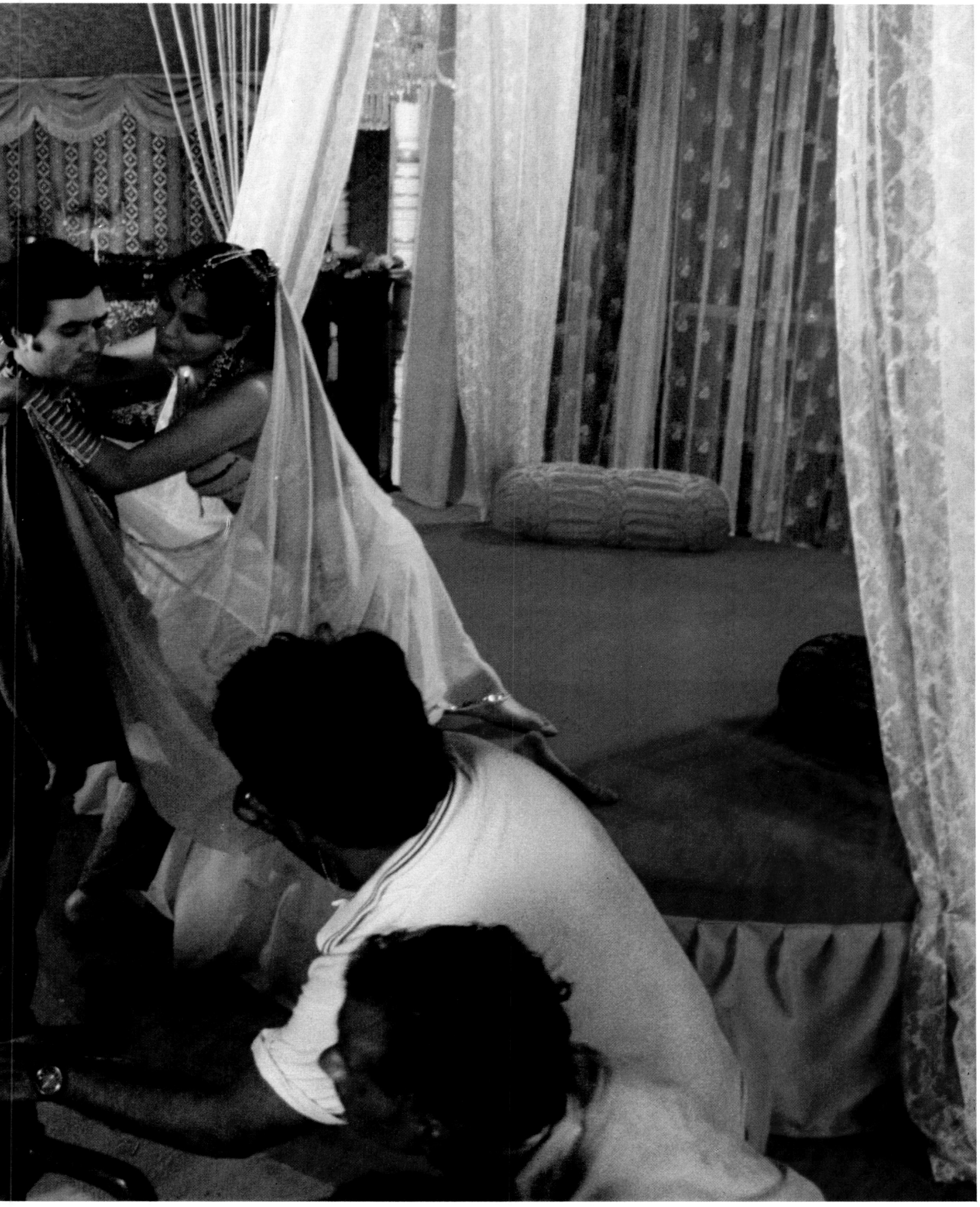

successes achieved by the internationally esteemed directors, or resulting from the solemn studies of the Poona graduates. These popular movies are a much criticized and often ridiculed phenomenon, so stereotyped that they are almost interchangeable: three hours of dancing, comedy, romance and fistfights, loosely tied to a plot (such as it is) that grinds to a halt every few minutes for the hero and heroine to burst into song. A typical scenario, into which all these ingredients are arbitrarily poured, might involve a village damsel running off briefly with a rich playboy before returning to the arms of the boy next door, a wife unjustly accused of adultery, or any sequence of events that could conceivably lead to a chase involving train, horse and helicopter.

The movies make no pretence at realism. They concentrate on satisfying the public's insatiable appetite for two-dimensional stories with a predictable mix of romance, melodrama and vicariously shared luxury; with sentimental partings that precede unlikely but happy endings; and flawlessly innocent heroes and heroines who are pitted against totally evil villains. Incorporating, as they still do, ornate language and formal action, Hindi films have not completely shed the effects of their origin as an imitation of traditional theatre.

Music, too, is indispensable. Its context in the story is almost irrelevant. Songs from the sound-tracks are widely advertised and are sometimes released for radio performance as long as a year before the film itself appears, becoming enormous hits and generating vast public interest in the forthcoming attraction. The lyric-writers are often well-known poets. Casting non-singing actors and actresses presents no problem: the numbers are invariably dubbed in by famous "playback singers", who are considered stars in their own right and whose records sell in huge numbers.

Indian comedians are not so much actors as slapstick comics, and the dialogues they are made to utter are sparse and smutty. As often as not, they get hopelessly drunk, stagger about, fall over chairs and into bathtubs, thereby delighting the audience, who have not come expecting witty repartee or sophisticated comment. In fact, there are very few Indian films where the dialogue is humorous in the Western sense. Comic players are much in demand, since almost every Hindi movie reserves time for their bits of business; but the convention has served to inhibit the development of intelligent comedy in the Indian cinema.

Many of the Hindi film industry's current shortcomings date from the Second World War when producers were ordered to devote one film in every three to Allied propaganda. There was little argument, since the government controlled the supply of raw film. At the same time, two things began to change the shape of Indian movies in general and Hindi productions in particular. The harsh economic climate meant that producers played safe by endlessly regurgitating the same tired old cinematic clichés. Furthermore, the shortage of venues—no new cinemas were

An agile dancer wearing a traditional costume gyrates for the camera against the unlikely backdrop of a modern, Western-style lounge. Most Hindi films are liberally endowed with romanticized song-and-dance interludes as essential ingredients for box-office success.

being built—meant that exhibitors and distributors could impose an almost tyrannical control over film content, and even dictate which stars should be cast by the producers.

It was the beginning of India's exaggerated "star system"—which, unlike Hollywood's, still prevails—and the price actors had to pay for such heady fame was the treadmill of having to work in as many as a dozen productions simultaneously. (Today's top stars may sign up for 20 or even 30 movies concurrently being filmed.) Entrepreneurs with currency to unload encouraged the proliferation of "mushroom" producers, who hired studios, stars and musicians and made up their movies as they went along. Infiltrating every channel of the industry was "black money": a complex mechanism for evading taxes by resorting to untraceable cash payments. The coming of Independence shortly after the war brought the industry no opportunity for relief. The government saw movies as an important source of revenue and eventually instituted taxes that came to represent over 50 per cent of all box-office receipts.

Censorship also has a long history. As early as 1919, an influx of films—mainly from the United States—sometimes presenting Westerners who were either drunk, abusive, scantily dressed or unfaithful to their spouses led to protests by British residents. London's *Westminster Gazette* went so far as to suggest that: "One of the great reasons for the hardly veiled contempt of the native Indians for us may be found in the introduction and development of moving pictures in India. It is difficult for the Britisher in India to keep up his dignity and to extol or enforce moral laws which the native sees lightly disregarded by the Britons themselves in the picture palaces."

The immediate result was the formation of a Board of Censors with offices in Bombay, Calcutta and Madras, authorized to license and certify movies, both home-grown and imported. The far-from-exemplary character of Westerners portrayed in movies turned out to be only one of their problems. A more serious consideration was the political aspirations of the Indians. The British, who ruled India, had failed to realize that many of the film-makers were nationalists, who were able to deliver their message by filming the many Indian myths and legends that involved the overthrow of some tyrannical ruler by a hero, or the exile of a native prince who eventually returned to claim his kingdom. The films were recognized by audiences as parables, in which the tyrants and usurpers represented the British. By the 1930s, the censors were removing many symbolic references to the movement for independence.

After Independence the character of the censorship changed; emphasis was on the suppression of overt sex, suggestiveness and the flouting of ancient traditions. Many of India's leaders were sincere but extremely puritanical men and extraordinary censorship regulations were imposed. Screen kisses were banned completely. Revealing costumes and move-

Cast members waiting to participate in a lavish production number rest between takes. Many who are involved in the big chorus scenes have studied classical Indian dance; but in popular Hindi films they are invariably called upon to perform a hybrid of ancient and modern steps to a fusion of Indian and Western music.

Observed by a large audience of guests and unoccupied studio staff, the cast of a typically lavish movie melodrama play a scene in which a glittering cardboard-and-plaster replica of a Hindu temple is being consecrated. Indian film scenarios often follow labyrinthine plot-lines combining love, adventure, social comment and domestic strife to an extreme of implausibility.

ments were forbidden to actresses because they were not in accordance with tradition (a view that was hardly compatible with ancient books like the *Kamasutra*, not to speak of erotic temple carvings) and the consumption of alcohol on the screen was also forbidden. The latter ruling was later modified by conceding that alcohol could be drunk on the screen but only by the more villainous characters in a film.

The script-writers, of course, found ways and means to circumvent the censors, but the result was a heavily suggestive eroticism that still pervades almost every Indian film. A popular scene that at one time recurred in almost every movie had the hero and heroine pursuing each other round trees; they would then be caught in a sudden downpour, or the heroine might fall into some unexpected river or lake. She would emerge from the rain or the river with her flimsy garments drenched, rendering them partially transparent and causing them to cling to the more obvious protuberances of her body. Another ploy was both simple and less of an imposition for the actress: when the script required her to serve her lover some kind of refreshment or simply to pick up something that had fallen to the floor, she bent towards the camera and afforded the audience a long look into her cleavage.

In the more permissive Seventies, rape scenes became popular. The heroine is menaced by the villain. She screams, fights, but is overpowered. Her sari is torn off and her *choli* is sufficiently ripped to expose much of her bosom. She is then hurled on to a bed, more or less ending the human involvement in the scene. The audience watch the rest of her garments fluttering to the floor, then the film cuts to a shot of, say, a piston rod in action. That is all: unless, before the piston starts to operate, the hero bursts in (more often than not, he does) to save his beloved.

To avoid the embargo on kissing, once the hero and rescued heroine are breathing heavily into each other's faces, the director may cut—more delicately than in the rape scenes—to two flowers swaying in the wind, their petals brushing. This is presumed to be artistic.

The tendency of Western films to become more explicit inevitably had its local effect and censorship gradually became more liberal. In 1978, in a film called *Satyam Shivam Sundaram* (Love Sublime), the censors finally relented and for the first time allowed a fully fledged kiss to appear on the screen. It helped to make the film—in most respects not so different from innumerable others—a stunning commercial success.

Making a film in Bombay is a long and involved process, attended by crisis, confusion and even farce, that puts one in mind of the most frenetic early days of Hollywood.

At the outset, the film has to be financed; and most of the time the producer will turn to the money-lenders, who are crouched spider-like in their dark, cobwebbed rooms in unlikely parts of the city. They are called

On location near Bombay, famed director Raj Kapoor discusses with the female lead the development of a scene in a multi-million-rupee production.

hoondiwallas—a *hoondi* being a note of hand—and, although they are by no means critics of film as an art form, they know a lot about their production. They know, for example, that a film will sell more on the names of the stars, and on those of the director and musical director, than on the story. The amount of money they are ready to part with will depend, therefore, on the stars the producer has tentatively managed to line up, and on his team of directors. The average financing for a film is between Rs 60 to 80 lakhs—a lakh being 100,000 rupees—or between $750,000 and $1 million. This money is not handed over all at once but in instalments; and the rate of interest may be as high as 60 per cent. There are other, more complicated ways to get the money. The producer can approach the distribution companies individually and persuade each one to assume a share of the cost in exchange for participation in the production profits. Or he can go to the Film Finance Corporation, sponsored by the government. The F.F.C. is the last resource of the producer. As a government body, it does not have much money to hand out and it is rather insistent on having an advance look at the non-existent script.

Neither the money-lender nor the producer is anxious to meet income-tax officials too frequently; hence the bulk of each hand-out is in cash. The actors—or, as they like to call themselves, artistes—are paid partly in "white money", by a cheque from the producer, and partly in "black money", by hard cash. A script-writer, a lyricist and a composer are signed up. The producer decides what his story is, the script-writer roughs out some lines and the film is ready to start. Then the *muhurat* (inauguration ceremony) takes place. An astrologer works out a promising date and time on which the shooting should start. On that date, the actors and everyone else who works on the film, as well as guests (usually from the Press), are present. In tribute, a garland is hung on the camera and a fresh coconut is broken in front of it. At the most auspicious second, the hero and heroine stand in front of the camera, the clapper-board is sounded, and the camera rolls for a few seconds to film a significant moment from the story. That ceremony completed, everyone eats sickly sweets for as long as he can bear it before trundling off home.

When the shooting schedule begins in earnest, the real pandemonium starts. Quite often the script for a given scene is ready only seconds before the camera must roll. The plot is not photographed in its actual sequence: the closing scenes may be shot at the start and the opening scenes at the end. Meanwhile, the principal actors are usually involved in several other films at the same time and, since the studios are always heavily booked by other film companies, dates have to be found on which all the actors as well as the studio are available simultaneously. These dates may be few and far between. Further lengthy delays may be caused by the producer's desperate attempt to raise more money. By the time the film is finally completed, five or six years may have elapsed since the auspicious date on which it started. It then has to pass the censors, a process that will take more time still. As a result of all this, the actors in an opening sequence that was shot last, quite often look considerably older than they do in the closing sequences.

Not long ago, I paid a visit to a Bombay film studio. To my surprise, the interior looked even more shabby than the exterior. It was during the monsoon season and the entrance corridors were smothered in mud brought in by the feet of people coming in off the rainy road. Even the walls seemed to drip. The studio floor itself was covered with dirty white cloth bearing many footprints; my guide and I had to take off our shoes before entering the set, which was crowded with grimy and unkempt technicians. The harassed director was busy with his electricians, arranging the positioning of the floor lighting. On shaky, unrailed, plywood catwalks high above the set, other sweaty technicians squatted, clutching arc lights and boom microphones.

The set itself consisted mainly of a vast, luxurious bed with a backdrop that displayed, through an inset window, large—and unlikely—snow-capped mountains. Two of the male stars, heavily made up and sporting false moustaches, were seated on hard wooden chairs awaiting the arrival of the young female star. She appeared at last wearing a yellow nylon nightie, climbed into bed and closed her eyes. With that, the two male stars moved into position, staring benevolently down at her from the foot of the bed. The camera started to whirr. Simultaneously, a prop mist poured in through the fake window, apparently drifting from the painted mountains beyond. The mist was in fact smoke and the special-effects man—clearly an enthusiast at his work—overdid it; in a matter of minutes the entire set had disappeared from view and everyone assembled in the studio was coughing violently.

When shooting finally resumed, the mist was under control; but the director had ordained that a fateful wind must blow through the window, carrying dead leaves into the bedroom. The whole set shuddered under a terrific blast from an off-camera wind machine. A forestful of dead leaves poured through the window to inundate actors, technicians and spectators alike. A false moustache fluttered past me. "Cut!" screamed the director. As I left, various minions were beginning the difficult task of sweeping up the leaves.

Although more Indian films than ever are being made, the popularity of the actors today seems quite precarious. A generation ago, the reputations of the great stars reached a zenith and remained there. Film after film starred famous names like Raj Kapoor, Dilip Kumar, Ashok Kumar, Dev Anand or Nargis—a star of the 1940s who was known as "The White Lady" because her saris were usually that colour. (White in India is not only a sign of sorrow but of purity, and Nargis normally played the part of

Diverted from their task of erecting stands for an exhibition elsewhere in the Taj Mahal Hotel, four Sikh workmen watch with fascination the parade of film celebrities and aspiring unknowns at a fund-raising party. A blasé guest from the party evidently does not share their interest.

a chaste and tragic woman.) Today movie stars of such permanent magnitude are far fewer.

Raj Kapoor has been one of the giants of the Bombay—and, indeed, the Indian—film world. The Kapoor family has dominated the film industry for decades: Raj's father, Prithviraj Kapoor, was a well-known film and stage actor—celebrated for his portrayals of Alexander the Great and the Mughal Emperor, Akbar—and also a member of the Indian Upper House of Parliament. Shashi, youngest brother of Raj, is well-known in the West as well as in India as an actor of saturnine good looks; in addition to coping with an enormously busy shooting schedule he has found time to set up, and make appearances at, a training school for young actors in Bombay. The third brother, Shammi, is successful as film producer and director as well as actor. Raj's elder son Randhir (usually known by his nickname Dabboo) plays an important part in running the studios founded by his father and he too is an influential producer-director in his own right.

Raj Kapoor himself emerged to fame after a career that began in the 1930s. As an actor, he specialized in vivid character roles and regarded himself as a kind of Indian Charlie Chaplin. He usually played opposite Nargis and the pair formed a team whose names together on a billboard established a guarantee of success for any movie. In time he began producing and directing his own films and, in 1952, founded his own studio—the "RK" in Bombay. Though perhaps not really a political person, Raj Kapoor's sympathies were supposedly with the masses, from whom his financial support came, and some of the films he made were much praised in the Soviet Union, where he was also personally very popular. One movie, *Awara* (The Vagabond)—in which he appeared with Nargis—became an enormous hit when it was released in the U.S.S.R. in 1954. His later films veered away from social commentary to pure escapist entertainment.

Nargis, now retired, married Sunil Dutt, another actor who functions as his own producer and director. In the late 1970s I visited the Dutts, whom my wife and I have known for many years, at their large rambling house on Pali Hill. Nargis herself started her career, as an adolescent, in 1942 and achieved fame with her very first film. In the next fifteen years she became legendary.

"Our films have changed a lot since I started," Nargis told me. "In 1942, for instance, actresses were thought of as people totally beyond the pale, who had loose morals. We weren't welcome socially. Then as more and more educated people came into films, our professional world gradually became more respectable.

"Today, to be in films here is *every* girl's ambition—but they all want to be 'stars', not actresses. And that's not unrealistic. Women are simply used as ornaments on the screen today, like dolls. They have nothing to

Bombayites queue outside a cinema showing the epic adventure film advertised on the huge billboard above their heads. Films are among the least expensive forms of entertainment in Bombay and seats can cost as little as 15 cents. Television in India is not widespread enough to offer any serious competition to the industry.

do except to look attractive for the men in the audience. And in Indian films it's very easy to be type-cast."

I met Ashok Kumar, one of the most famous of the older stars, on the set of a film and he made the same point. "I started my career in 1932," he said. "At first I was the hero; but naturally, as I grew older, I started to play character parts. As a hero, I had been required to do the same thing in every film and so I thought character parts would be a challenge. Not so. In every film I used to be cast as the heroine's father and he always said the same things. Then I got older still and they began to cast me as the heroine's grandfather, and the same thing happened all over again!

"Sometimes it is hard to remember which bits of dialogue go into which film. But usually, even if you say your lines from one film when you are shooting in another, it doesn't make too much difference."

As far back as 1939, there were 68 film magazines in India. Most of them were published in English and emanated from Bombay. For a number of years the most famous of these was *Filmindia*, a magazine devoted largely to gossip and innuendo about the current stars, but also to long and solemn articles about how to improve the standard of Indian cinema. More such magazines came along—some, like *Filmfare*, started by companies that already published newspapers and other magazines, and thus had powerful financial backing. *Filmfare* emerged as the leading publication in the movie field and *Filmindia* ceased publication in the late 1950s. Today an enormous number of mass-circulation magazines are devoted to the industry. They are uncountable, in the sense that some mushroom into the sunlight one day and are dead the next. Overwhelmingly, they are gossipy, full of stories about eventful parties attended by the stars—who quarrelled with whom, who got drunk, who made an amorous pass at whom, or indeed at what.

Film stars are perennially among the highest earners in Bombay. A top star may receive Rs 20 lakhs for each movie—and the black-money share of their earnings means that their take-home pay, after taxes, is disproportionately high. They drink imported Scotch, drive luxurious foreign cars, and maintain large and expensive households. Typically, their houses are a curious mixture of Eastern and Western extravagances: gilt and chrome bars, psychedelic décor, and huge beds—canopied and mirrored, with black silk sheets. They buy valuable modern paintings but also decorate their walls with flights of china ducks, and keep kewpie dolls on their tables, as well as tourist souvenirs brought back from every country they have ever visited.

The film magazines make much mileage out of the alleged wild social affairs that are supposed to take place all the time; actually, when the top stars throw parties in their own houses, they almost always invite the Press, thus putting everyone on their best behaviour. "They are very boring

Short Cuts to Illusion

Given the right cinematic ingredients—star names, romance and plenty of action— Bombay film audiences not only disregard a stereotyped plot or cliché-ridden script, but also turn a blind eye to blatant visual imperfections. Rather than shoot a film on location, a director may use a less-than-convincing fake townscape (right) on a set, where sound and action can be better controlled. And to save on the cost of hiring actors, a producer may feature cardboard "extras" for long shots in crowd scenes, though the result appears incongruous when seen close up, beside a flesh-and-blood human being (below).

Such devices do not provoke disbelief even when the same props are repeated in different films. In fact, their very familiarity— like that of the stock situations around which most plots are built—may help to create the self-contained dream world that Bombay cinema-goers are addicted to.

Tens of thousands of enthusiastic Bombayites surround a convoy of trucks carrying idolized Indian movie stars. The celebrities are lending their glamorous presence to help raise funds for a campaign to aid cyclone victims.

parties," a film journalist told me. "Everybody talks about his own new films."

India's film stars generally seem to have few close friends outside their own closed circle. In fact, as Parveen Babi, a young actress who has had a rather tempestuous life, told me, most stars have none at all apart from their yes-men (in Hindi known as *chamchas* or spoons), of whom each top actor has an entourage.

There are rather more than a hundred cinemas in Bombay, not a large number in proportion to the population; but for each one of the permanent cinemas in the main part of the city, there are perhaps half a dozen travelling theatres that take films around to the outlying areas, making them available to the poor in their *chawls* and shanty colonies. The films are screened in marquees erected for the occasion and, though these movies are unlikely to be current hits, ticket prices are low enough —well below a rupee—to make it possible for most people to attend. Many of Bombay's unmarried office workers—the audiences are always predominantly male—go to the cinema every night.

Films made in Bombay are distributed in many other parts of the world —especially Britain, Europe and the United States—where there are colonies of Indians. But the Bombay distributors also sell in, for instance, North Africa, the Middle East and Eastern Europe, where the films, dubbed or subtitled, are imported for general public consumption. Once, on a repulsively cold day in the wilds of an Eastern European country, I was introduced to some peasants. An old man, the head of the community, said something to my interpreter. "I told him you came from India," the interpreter informed me. "He says it is a very good country and has produced one very great man." The old peasant snapped his knobbly fingers, trying to remember the name. "Gandhi?" I suggested helpfully. No, it wasn't Gandhi. "Nehru?" Not him either. Suddenly, the name came back to the old man. "Raj Kapoor," he said.

The universality of the Hindi films stems from the fact that they restrict themselves to cultural common denominators, to broad characterizations and obvious story lines. However, the unavoidable compromises imposed by this consideration on the taste and originality of the films leave the popular Hindi cinema open to ceaseless criticism—much of it highly deserved; and the directors often lay the blame at the door of the unsophisticated audiences, whoever they may be, who demand a constant diet of implausible excitement, glamour and luxury. The director Dabboo Kapoor once expressed himself emphatically to me on the subject: "In some cities there is no entertainment for the people except films. They will take any rubbish they are offered, but they prefer some kinds of rubbish to others. They like music, songs, dances, sex, fighting. You mix it all up and offer it to them, and they will take it. They don't want to look at serious films because their own lives are so miserable. We give them what they want."

In the words of one commentator, perhaps the people should not be faulted for preferring films that "emphasize aspiration rather than reality". You can see the intense anticipation in the light that falls from the street-lamps across the faces of the people in the endless queues—the faces of addicts, tired but expectant of a panacea against the heat, the boredom, the anxieties of poverty.

Once inside the large foyer, its chipped and peeling walls painted pink, they buy their tickets and shuffle to their seats. An uncarpeted, concrete floor lies beneath their feet. Fans on the wall shift the warm air around them and, amidst the susurrations of breath from their neighbours, they await their three-hour escape from reality into a dreamland that unites them in an unacknowledged community, stronger than that of the city itself.

Ordeal by Flood

As the rains teem down, people struggle knee-deep through an inundated street in Breach Candy, an area in the west of the city that faces the Arabian Sea.

When Bombay's four-month monsoon season begins in early June, the torrential rains bring long-awaited relief from the oppressive summer heat of 90°F or higher. But in the many low-lying areas of the city, flooding is an inevitable consequence. An average of 24 inches of rain falls during the month of July alone; and when prolonged downpours coincide with a tide high enough to close the outlets of the city's drainage conduits, streets can remain awash for hours at a time, disrupting road and rail traffic, and keeping workers from their offices and children from school. Yet most Bombayites face their annual ordeal with a composure that is born of long familiarity. Grasping large umbrellas, they wade about their business—sometimes troubling to tuck up the hems of their saris or *dhotis*, but more often simply ignoring the waters that lap around their legs.

Railway road-beds become pedestrian walkways when floods block trains.

Flood waters submerge a low-lying section of thoroughfare, bringing traffic to a halt. Vehicles at a slightly higher level (background) can still manoeuvre.

Waterlogged commuters scramble to board a bus. Flooding brings delays and cuts in service, causing long waits and crowding in the few buses that can operate.

Schoolboys cope good-humouredly as water rises above gumboot level.

Holding brief-case and bag clear of the deluge, Bombayites press on to work.

His dhoti tucked up neatly, a man wades across a road in Breach Candy.

A city employee guards a signposted hazard: a manhole without a cover.

On a road in the northern area of Parel, a taxi-driver attempts temporary repairs to his stranded cab while a policeman patiently directs traffic around it.

A carrier's bullock-powered cart proves more reliable than motor transport in the flooded streets.

Thigh-high in the deluge, determined Bombayites cross paths by a Breach Candy school that caters for the children of German diplomats and businessmen.

Bibliography

Barnouw, Erik, and Krishnaswamy, S., *Indian Film.* Columbia University Press, New York, 1963.
Basham, A. L., *A Cultural History of India.* Clarendon Press, Oxford, 1975.
Bence-Jones, Mark, *Palaces of the Raj.* George Allen & Unwin Ltd., London, 1973.
Bhattacharya, S., *A Dictionary of Indian History.* University of Calcutta, Calcutta, 1967.
Boman-Behram, B. K., *The Decline of Bombay.* Conway Private Ltd., Bombay, 1969.
Bombay Metropolitan Regional Planning Board, *Regional Plan for Bombay Metropolitan Region, 1970-91.* Government of Maharashtra, Poona, 1974.
Booch, Harish S., *Pocket Guide to Bombay.* The Lakhani Book Depot, Bombay, 1954.
Bulsara, J. F., *Patterns of Social Life in Metropolitan Areas.* The Gujarat Research Society, Bombay, 1970.
Cameron, James, *Indian Summer.* Macmillan & Co. Ltd., London, 1974.
Chamberlain, M. E., *Britain and India: The Interaction of Two Peoples.* David & Charles Ltd., Newton Abbot, Devon, 1974.
Chatterjee, A. K., *Contemporary Urban Architecture in Bombay.* The Macmillan Co. of India Ltd., Delhi and Bombay, 1977.
Chaudhuri, Nirad C., *Hinduism.* Chatto & Windus Ltd., London, 1979.
Costa, Benedict, *Bombay: The Twilight Zone.* Hind Pocket Books Ltd., Delhi, 1972.
Dobbin, Christine, *Urban Leadership in Western India: Politics and Communities in Bombay City 1840-1885.* Oxford University Press, Oxford, 1972.
Edwardes, S. M., *The Rise of Bombay.* Reprinted Vol. X of The Census of India Series, The Times of India Press, Bombay, 1902.
Edwardes, S. M., *The Gazetteer of Bombay City and Island (3 vols.).* The Times Press, Bombay, 1909-10.
Ennis, John, *Bombay Explosion.* Cassell & Co. Ltd., London, 1959.
Fodor, Eugene, and Curtis, William, eds., *Fodor's India 1976/77.* Hodder & Stoughton Ltd., London, 1977.
Fortescue, John, *Narrative of the visit to India of their Majesties King George V and Queen Mary.* Macmillan & Co. Ltd., London, 1912.
Gibbons, Suzanne, and Steinmetz, Hazel, eds., *Bombay Handbook.* Tata Press Ltd., Bombay, 1977.
Greenwall, Harry J., *The Aga Khan.* The Cresset Press, London, 1952.
Hiro, Dilip, *Inside India Today.* Routledge & Kegan Paul Ltd., London, and Boston, Mass., 1978.
Johnson, B. L. C., *India, Resources and Development.* Heinemann Educational Books Ltd., London, 1976.
Johnson, Donald and Jean, *God and Gods in Hinduism.* Arnold Heinemann, New Delhi, 1972.
Khan, Aga, *Memoirs, World Enough and Time.* Cassell & Co. Ltd., London, 1954.
Kincaid, Dennis, *British Social Life in India 1608-1937.* Routledge & Kegan Paul Ltd., London, 1973.
Lewis, Reba, *Three Faces has Bombay.* The Popular Book Depot, Bombay, 1957.
Malabari, Phiroze B. M., *Bombay in the Making.* T. Fisher Unwin, London, 1910.
Mehta, Vinod, *Bombay: A Private View.* Thacker & Co. Ltd., Bombay, 1971.
Naipaul, V. S., *An Area of Darkness.* André Deutsch Ltd., London, 1964.
Nanavutty, Piloo, *The Parsees.* National Book Trust, India, New Delhi, 1977.
Nyrop, Richard F., *Area Handbook for India.* Foreign Area Studies of the American University, Washington, D.C., 1975.
Pandey, B. N., *The Break-up of British India.* Macmillan & Co. Ltd., London, 1969.
Punekar, Vijaya B., *The Son Kolis of Bombay.* G. R. Bhatkal for Popular Book Depot, Bombay, 1959.
Rangoonwalla, Firoze, *75 Years of Indian Cinema.* Indian Book Co., New Delhi, 1975.
Rau, Santha Rama, and the Editors of Time-Life Books, *The Cooking of India.* Time-Life International (Nederland) B.V., 1977.
Rowland, Benjamin, *The Art and Architecture of India.* Penguin Books Ltd., Harmondsworth, Middlesex, 1976.
Selbourne, David, *An Eye to India.* Penguin Books Ltd., Harmondsworth, Middlesex, 1977.
Sen, K. M., *Hinduism.* Penguin Books Ltd., Harmondsworth, Middlesex, 1969.
Sheppard, Samuel T., *Bombay.* The Times of India Press, Bombay, 1932.
Smith, Vincent A., *The Oxford History of Modern India (1740-1947).* Clarendon Press, Oxford, 1970.
Spate, O. H. K., and Learmonth, A. T. A., *India and Pakistan.* Methuen & Co. Ltd., London, 1967.
Stamp, Gavin, *Victorian Bombay: Urbs Prima in Indis.* Art & Archaeology Research Papers, London, 1977.
Walker, Benjamin, *Hindu World (2 vols.).* George Allen & Unwin Ltd., London, 1968.
Wilkinson, Theon, *Two Monsoons.* Duckworth & Co. Ltd., London, 1976.
Williams, L. F. Rushbrook, *A Handbook for Travellers in India, Pakistan, Nepal, Bangladesh and Sri Lanka.* John Murray Ltd., London, 1975.
Woodruff, Philip, *The Men Who Ruled India (2 vols.).* Jonathan Cape Ltd., London, 1963.
Yule, Henry, and Burnell, Arthur Coke, *Hobson-Jobson (A Glossary of Anglo-Indian Colloquial Words and Phrases).* John Murray Ltd., London, 1886.

Acknowledgements and Picture Credits

The editors wish to thank the following for their valuable assistance: Max Caulfield, London; Asit Chandmal, Bombay; Dr. John Compton; Susie Dawson, London; François Geoffrey Dechaume, Paris; William Donaldson, London; Government of India Tourist Office, London; Ali Peter John, Bombay; Shashi Kapoor, Bombay; Miss Mahalaxmi, Bombay; Zareer Masani, London; David Matthews, London; Russell Miller, London; Prakash Mirchandani, London; Leela Moraes, New Delhi; Dr. B. N. Pandey, London University; Jayant Patel, Diwana Bhel-Poori House, London; Shirin Patel, Bombay; Perrot Phillips, London; Susan de la Plain, London; Florence Prouverelle, New Delhi; Raghu Rai, New Delhi; Prem Sagar, Bombay; Sita Ram Sharma, London; Olga Tellis, Bombay; Giles Wordsworth, London.

Sources for pictures in this book are shown below. Credits for the pictures from left to right are separated by commas; from top to bottom by dashes.

All photographs are by Bruno Barbey except: Pages 10, 11—British Museum, photo by Chris Barker. 16, 17—Map by Hunting Surveys Ltd., London (Silhouettes by Norman Bancroft-Hunt, Caterham Hill, Surrey). 22—W. W. Hooper from the John Hillelson Collection. 38, 39—Paul Popper Ltd., London. 46, 47 (plus inset)—India Office Library and Records. 50, 51—Tata Services Ltd., Bombay. 51 (inset)—Pennwick Publishing Inc., New York. 53—India Office Library and Records. 78—Jehangir Gazdar from Susan Griggs Picture Agency, London. 82, 83—Jehangir Gazdar from Susan Griggs Picture Agency, London. 111—Asit Chandmal. 123—Frederic V. Grunfeld. 125—Jehangir Gazdar from Susan Griggs Picture Agency, London.

Index

Numerals in italics indicate a photograph or drawing of the subject mentioned.

Colour reproduction by Irwin Photography Ltd., at their Leeds Studio.
Filmsetting by C. E. Dawkins (Typesetters) Ltd., London, SE1 1UN.
Printed and bound in Italy by Arnoldo Mondadori, Verona.

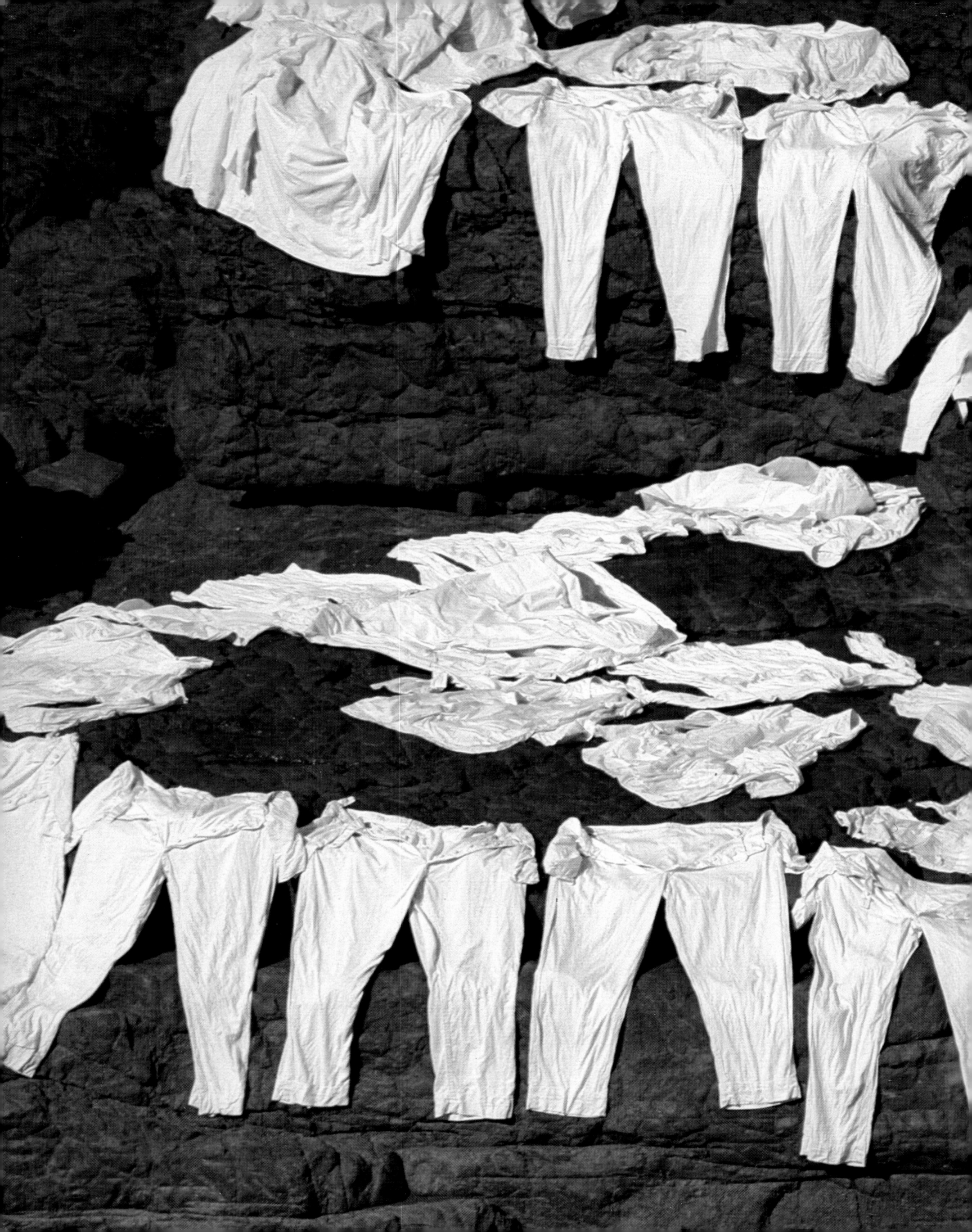